A New Owner's
Guide to
BOXERS

JG-103

Overleaf: Adult and puppy Boxers owned and bred by the author, Rick Tomita.
Opposite page: Pal and Abel bred by Vancroft Kennels, courtesy of Marcia Adams.

The Publisher wishes to acknowledge the following owners of the dogs in this book: Marcia Adams, Steven and Ann Anderson, Les Baker, Susan Bendziewicz, Richard Berry, Carol Beusee, Sam and Win Bitler, Hope and Barry Blazer, D. Brace and R. Olifent-Brace, Dianne and Dennis Bradshaw, Ralf Brinkman, Sandra Carter, Deborah Clark, Ella M. DuPree, Ingrid Feder of Fiero Boxers, Pete Foster, Nicole Haineault, the Heldenbrands, Carol Hessels, Judy Horton, Verena Jaeger, Shozo Kawakami, Adam Koester, Jeannie and Bruce Korson, Lucie Lecomte, Sieglinde Lehman, Nell Marshall, Jeff and Missy Mathis, the Michals family, Brigitie Miller, Laura Miller, Yvonne Miller, Natalie Robbins, David and Patti Ann Rutledge, Cynthia Idzile-Starr and Paul Starr, Xena Takahashi, Tim Teubner, Jo Thomson, Rick Tomita, Dr. and Mrs. William Truesdale, Brian and Janine Westenberger, Cynthia S. White, Margaret and Frank Wildman.

Photographers: John Ashbey, Susan Bendziewicz, Mary Bloom, Paulette Braun, Tara Darling, Isabelle Francais, Judy Iby, Photography by Marcia, Tobé Saskor, Robert Smith, E. Takahashi, Karen Taylor.

The author acknowledges the contribution of Judy Iby for the following chapters: Sport of Purebred Dogs, Identification and Finding the Lost Dog, Traveling with Your Dog, Behavior and Canine Communication; and Health Care for Your Dog.

Distributed in the UNITED STATES to the Pet Trade by T.F.H. Publications, Inc., One T.F.H. Plaza, Neptune City, NJ 07753; distributed in the UNITED STATES to the Bookstore and Library Trade by National Book Network, Inc. 4720 Boston Way, Lanham MD 20706; in CANADA to the Pet Trade by H & L Pet Supplies Inc., 27 Kingston Crescent, Kitchener, Ontario N2B 2T6; Rolf C. Hagen Inc., 3225 Sartelon St. Laurent-Montreal Quebec H4R 1E8; in CANADA to the Book Trade by Vanwell Publishing Ltd., 1 Northrup Crescent, St. Catharines, Ontario L2M 6P5 ; in ENGLAND by T.F.H. Publications, PO Box 15, Waterlooville PO7 6BQ; in AUSTRALIA AND THE SOUTH PACIFIC by T.F.H. (Australia), Pty. Ltd., Box 149, Brookvale 2100 N.S.W., Australia; in NEW ZEALAND by Brooklands Aquarium Ltd. 5 McGiven Drive, New Plymouth, RD1 New Zealand; in Japan by T.F.H. Publications, Japan—Jiro Tsuda, 10-12-3 Ohjidai, Sakura, Chiba 285, Japan; in SOUTH AFRICA by Lopis (Pty) Ltd., P.O. Box 39127, Booysens, 2016, Johannesburg, South Africa. Published by T.F.H. Publications, Inc.
MANUFACTURED IN THE
UNITED STATES OF AMERICA
BY T.F.H. PUBLICATIONS, INC.

A New Owner's
Guide to
BOXERS

Rick Tomita

Contents

The Boxer is a noble and elegant breed.

Boxer puppies are adorable and playful. ↵

Boxers are athletic and coordinated, performing very well at agility trials and the like.

The name Boxer comes from the way the breed "puts up its dukes" when playing.

Handlers must be familiar with the Boxer breed standard.

INTRODUCTION to the Boxer

I like many of you fondly recall the Boxer of my youth. Thus, it was not surprising that I again selected the breed as an adult. As an established breeder, I have interviewed hundreds of prospective Boxer owners over the last 20+ years and, more often than not, they have grown up with the breed.

That the Boxer has long been a favored family pet is not surprising. Boxers and children seem to be made for each other. Both are eager, enthusiastic, energetic and fun loving. Parents appreciate the short, low-maintenance coat, moderate size and sweet, stable temperament.

Although the name may suggest otherwise, the Boxer is a lover not a fighter. This is Brazilian Ch. Warena's Amadeus.

However, it should be remembered that Boxers, like children, have an inquisitive nature. However, a house that is Boxer-proof is also child-proof.

Though Boxers are generally people friendly and inordinately fond of kissing, they will protect if the situation presents itself. Historically, they have been used in war and police work. They have also excelled as Seeing Eye™/service dogs and in therapy situations.

The breed has also stood out in the dog show ring. Not only have they earned championship titles but have gone on to achieve record-setting wins.

Boxers and children seem to be made for each other. Both are eager, enthusiastic, and fun-loving. This is Jacquet's Kaiser owned by Shozo Kawakami, Japan.

Obedience titles are not as numerous, but have been regularly earned by those dedicated to the breed and that field of endeavor.

Owners of the breed appreciate its short, low-maintenance coat, moderate size and sweet and stable temperament. This is Ch. Vihabra's Sun Tan with owner Xena Takahashi.

While it may appear that the Boxer has a little something for everyone all contained in the same package, it is not a breed that should be brought into the home without some research and careful consideration. Not all people nor all lifestyles are compatible with Boxer ownership.

Boxers are generally people-friendly and inordinately fond of kissing. This Boxer pup is owned by Steven and Ann Anderson.

In the pages that follow, I have put together a brief overview of the breed. This is meant only as an introduction for the prospective or new owner of a Boxer. Much more detailed information is available in companion works such as *The World of the Boxer* by yours truly, Richard Tomita, as well as others written by experienced and knowledgeable breed fanciers.

The importance of good breeding cannot be stressed enough. This is Ch. Jacquet's Vacheron; sire of the very smart Bosco Michals.

The Boxer has long been a favorite family pet. This is Bosco with owner George Michals.

BEST OF WINNERS

BURLINGTON COUNTY
KENNEL CLUB
1996

ASHREY PHOTO
BY BARBARA

ORIGINS of the Boxer

The Boxer is descended from the ancient molosser-type breeds that once existed in many parts of the world including most of Europe and Asia. These dogs were of medium to large size, powerful and often aggressive. They were of a generalized type or family of dogs that had yet to become fixed into specific breeds. If you visualize a triangle with the Mastiffs of Tibet at the uppermost point, the molosser-type dogs would be the first step toward formation of most of the working breeds we know today, the Boxer among them.

The second step in breed formation was the division of the molosser types into two recognizable groups. One consisted of large dogs with long to semi-long coats in a variety of colors. These would later become the flock guardian dogs that include the Great Pyrenees, Kuvasz and Komondor, as well as a variety of internationally recognized breeds that have not yet attained American Kennel Club (AKC) recognition. The second group consisted of large- to medium-sized dogs with short coats in colors of blue, fawn or brindle. The English Mastiff, Bulldog, Bullmastiff, Great Dane and Boxer would ultimately develop from this group.

The next evolutionary step, from the 12th to 14th century, was a further division of the short-coated molossers in Central and Western Europe, as well as in Southern France, Spain and Italy. Depending upon their functional qualities, three distinct lines developed:

1) a heavier type of dog that was the precursor of the English Mastiff (England), Neapolitan Mastiff (Italy) and the Dogue de Bordeaux (France);

2) a large dog with longer legs which produced the Great Dane (Germany), the Irish Wolfhound (Ireland) and the Scottish Deerhound (Scotland);

3) A smaller, lighter dog with greater agility that had a short, massive head that would one day identify the bull-type breeds such as the Bulldog (England), the Cane Corso (Italy) and the Boxer (Germany).

The three evolutionary lines continued to develop based solely on function characteristics. As particular structural features proved vital to specific tasks, they were selectively bred again and again. In this manner, breeds were eventually developed.

The German dogs of this period were differentiated only as to function. The names by which they were known were determined by the work which they performed, for example the Bullenbeisser (bull biter) and

A painting of the Bullenbeissers from the 18th century by J.E.L. Reidinger of Augsburg.

Berenbeisser (bear biter). While the Bullenbeisser and the Berenbeisser were essentially the same dog, they had been named differently due to function rather than form.

The Bullenbeisser has been described as a medium sized dog with very strong muscles and bones, a not long but squarish head, extremely strong mandibles, of a very courageous, brave, competitive spirit and of an extremely loyal character.

Through selective breeding, the Bullenbeisser was reduced in size. This smaller dog can be seen in the paintings of J.E.L. Reidinger of Augsburg (1698-1767). The head is typical of the Boxer while the body shows the same general outline. Initially, these smaller Bullenbeissers came only in colors of fawn or brown brindle with black masks. It was not until about 1830 that the white markings appeared, which have been attributed to the introduction of English Bulldogs into the breeding programs. However, the Bulldogs of that era were not the stylized versions seen today, but were of a more mastiff-type structure that was consistent with the functional aspects of the Bullenbeisser with which they were bred.

It was not until the latter part of the 19th century that the German people began to appreciate the value of this smaller mastiff-type dog that had been used for hunting and fighting. Long after the interest in linebreeding other breeds was employed, the concept of producing dogs that were not only functional but also pleasing to the eye began to be seen in the Bullenbeisser. The final step, which led to the Boxer we know today, occurred in 1895 in Munich, where a dog named Flocki was entered in an experimental dog show class. Flocki was a product of a Bullenbeisser breeding to an English Bulldog. Only in the head and expression does he resemble today's Boxer. However, it was these characteristics that led to his registration as the #1 Boxer in the book of records.

While the early dogs lacked homogeneity, their contribution to the breed as a whole was important as each one had predominant Boxer features in development. Among these early registered dogs, four stand out: two females known as Blanka Von Argentor and Meta v.d. Passage; and two males known as Wotan and Flock St. Salvator. These four originated two distinct lines: one descending from Wotan that possessed marked type and great strength; the other from Flock St.

The early Boxer Flock St. Salvator. The first breed standard was based on this dog.

12

Meta v.d. Passage was among the four early Boxers that contributed greatly to the breed and laid the real foundation from which it would develop. Salvator that were of square and elegant build, though rather light in head. The subsequent union of these two lines laid the real foundation from which the Boxer as a breed would develop.

The first German Boxer Club was founded in January 1896 followed shortly thereafter by their first official Boxer show in March of the same year. The debate regarding the written standard began at that show and continued until January 14, 1902 when a standard based upon Flock St. Salvator was adopted.

Although it is generally accepted that the Boxer is of German origin, the name is English. There are two theories, first that the word "Boxer" is a corruption of the word "Boxl" which had been previously applied to various dogs in Germany. The second theory is that the name derived from the characteristic way the Boxer uses his front paws when playing or fighting.

HISTORY in Germany

by Karla Spitzer

The period 1902-1911 was a period of growth and development for the breed. Greater homogeneity was achieved within the breed. In addition, a number of less desirable traits became breed disqualifications through revisions of the written standard.

While many of the early dogs were white or parti-colored, by 1904 solid black was a disqualification. The only reason anyone would give as to why this color was targeted for deletion was due to the "unacceptable behavior" of a man referred to only as Herr Schactner, the owner of the black Graf Blitz von Graudenz.

The color white remained registrable for a much longer time. Then, around 1925-1936, white was frowned upon. Various speculations have been made as to why whites fell out of favor. Some say that it was to distinguish them from the English Bulldog, while others cite that as the use of the Boxer as a police dog increased, the white color was too easy to see at night. Whatever the reason, both black and white Boxers remain disqualifications in all Boxer standards.

Firmly planted on America's eastern coast, this Boxer looks across the vast Atlantic remembering its German origins.

At any rate, by 1911, when the future Frau Stockmann, whose story embodies the history of the breed in Germany, came onto the dog scene in Munich, the breed was well on its way to becoming popular in Germany.

The then-Friederun Miram had dreamed all her young life of owning a Boxer, a breed she had only seen a picture of in one of her brother's books. On the spot she had fallen totally, instantly and permanently in love.

She left home in her late teens to further her

education and everything she did thereafter had something to do with Boxers. Whether through art, photography or the show ring, her knowledge and understanding of the breed were legendary even in her own time.

While her initial association with Philip Stockmann was merely a dutiful social obligation, someone with whom she was expected to have dinner once a month, this quickly changed when he presented her with his beloved dog, Pluto, a large brindle Boxer male. However romantic this might seem today, fate was a mixed blessing. Pluto became known as "The Hellhound." He was dog-aggressive in the extreme, unmanageable on a leash, with a tendency to run away and attack other animals. However, Frau Stockmann was not easily deterred and loved Pluto passionately.

Pluto was a good enough Boxer, "of the old type," to be entered in the stud book. Thus, he became her kennel's first entry under the "von Dom" prefix. The name derives

Philip Stockmann with sentry dogs. During World War I Boxers were used to assist the German Home Guard against snipers firing on soldiers during guard duty.

"The Mother of the Boxer," Friederun Stockmann feeding her famous von Dom Boxers. In the 20th century she established herself as a breeder, exhibitor and artist in the dog world.

from Frau Stockmann's recollection of the many fights Pluto had had in the vicinity of the cathedral (Dom). However, in spite of Pluto, the name "von Dom" would become world famous among Boxer lovers.

Not long after, the future Frau Stockman purchased Laska with the money her parents had been paying for expensive art lessons. One thing led to another and she ultimately married Philip Stockman. Subsequently they rented a house outside of Munich and established themselves as Boxer breeders. It was during this time that she acquired the champion, Roll von Vogelsberg, who became the stud for her Laska. Later she would acquire a champion bitch, Urschi von Hildesberg.

During the years preceding World War I, things continued to go well for the Stockmanns. Frau Stockmann established herself not only as a breeder and exhibitor but also an artist in the dog world. Her carvings and photography were successful and much sought after.

By 1914, the Stockmanns had a growing and successful kennel and a baby daughter on their new farm. However, Austria was about to declare war, which Germany would soon join. Within weeks, Philip was "drafted" and Frau Stockmann was alone.

Later that year, the Boxer Club in Munich began a campaign to mobilize all usable Boxers to assist the German Home Guard against snipers and other enemy infiltrators who were firing on soldiers during guard duty. Upon a recommendation from one of Frau Stockmann's old friends, Philip was contacted as a breeder of Boxers. Thus it was that the Boxer became a pioneer war dog.

While both trained champions and pets were utilized by the army, the champions were the first to be taken. This is not as unusual as it may sound in that the requirement for a championship in Germany, then and now, was a demonstration of working ability. This was equivalent to what we would call *Schutzhund* work today.

Boxers, with their great speed, agility and power, proved invaluable. Sniper attacks dropped dramatically once soldiers began patrolling with Boxers. Later, other breeds were also used, but in the

Frau Stockmann's Champion Sigurd von Dom at 14 months of age, the first Boxer she had ever sold to an American.

beginning, Boxers were the principle war dogs of Germany. One of the finest was the Champion Roll von Vogelsberg. His unerring nose and instinct made it possible for him to round up and hold whole groups of smugglers and snipers by himself until human help arrived.

International Champion Lustig von Dom being shown by Frau Stockmann in Germany.

In spite of the war, Roll still managed to sire a litter or two for Frau Stockmann, producing a number of famous offspring. Although, the day-to-day reality of running a kennel and army during the war was just plain misery, Frau Stockmann persevered even when many of her most promising dogs had to be sold or fell ill from lack of money and adequate veterinary services. Heartening was the fact that Roll, in spite of his age and the long hard years of war, won a fifth championship after the war, allowing Frau Stockmann to retire him undefeated.

Life following the war was not much better, but being an indomitable personality, Frau Stockmann managed to breed the sire of her new dynasty during this time. Ivein von Dom, a red fawn, while not a champion himself, sired Champion Sigurd von Dom and International Champion Pia von Isebeck. Then, in 1933, she produced Lustig von Dom, who would "put everything else in the shade," as she put it later. Initially, she had thought Lustig was a "cheap pup" because of the white markings on his face. In German terms, he was faulted for the pink on his nose and muzzle.

As the "dog game" and life in Germany began to once again flourish, Lustig went on to become a champion. During this time many wealthy Americans came to Frau Stockmann to buy dogs as her reputation as a knowledgeable and impeccable breeder spread. While she turned down many offers for Lustig, she did sell Sigurd, at five years of age, to Mrs. William Z. Breed. Ultimately, however, tragedy was destined to strike again as the Third Reich began to gain power in Germany. Having no other choice, Lustig was sold to the Tugley Wood Kennels owned by Erwin O. Freund. He arrived in the United States in March 1937 and earned his championship within a week of his first show.

As painful as the sale of Lustig was for Frau Stockman, he was of great benefit for the U.S. Boxers. Lustig's line eventually produced the illustrious Bang Away of Sirrah Crest.

This is Jahrsjugendchampion Impala v. Okeler Forst, SchH I, AD, bred and owned by Ralf Brinkman, Germany.

After Lustig's departure there were a few more years of peace and prosperity. But gradually Germany drifted closer to its role in World War II and more and more matters were taken over and regulated by the government. Finally, the German government created a department of "German Dog Affairs" which was controlled by the Army High Command. Large dog shows were forbidden, though, for some reason, small ones were not. It was anticipated that dogs would once again be required for military purposes and regulations were passed that required at least one parent of any given mating have a medal for obedience in order to ensure that the offspring would be trainable. Once this program was implemented, all the

This is Int. Ch. Patrick v. Stedinger Hof, SchH III, AD, owned by Ralf Brinkman, Germany.

dogs were reviewed and only the obedience-trained dogs received food rations.

Boxers were ranked second in terms of desirability, probably because of their record in World War I. The German Shepherd Dog was always ranked first because, as Frau Stockmann lamented, they could be trained by anyone, unlike the intelligent and sometimes stubborn Boxer, and their coats gave them better protection against the cold.

With the outbreak of World War II, Frau Stockmann was once again in desperate straits trying to feed and care for her dogs. However, she maintained a training program of tracking, obedience and Schutzhund to meet future needs of the army. She also trained messenger dogs for use behind and around enemy lines.

Following the end of the war and the loss of her husband in 1945, Frau Stockmann restarted her breeding program. Several of Lustig's progeny had been whisked out of Germany and into America following the outbreak of war. These included his son, the Champion Kyrras von der Bluteneau, and his sister, Liesel von der Bluteneau. Others included Ajax von der Holderburg and littermate Arno von der Holderburg and Xuntfig and Volkman von Dom. Of Lustig's top class sons, only one, Danilo von Konigsee, remained in Germany.

Post-war litters were disappointing as the years of hardship and deprivation took their toll. While all other puppies were dying, Frau Stockmann took a major risk in breeding her Anka von Hofbauer, her most promising bitch, to the German Champion Harry von der Storchenburg. Nine weeks later, Anka whelped a litter. She was the only bitch to rear her litter during this time.

Four years later, in 1949, it was the Americans that helped reestablish the von Dom kennels from the progeny of the dogs previously purchased from Frau Stockmann's kennel. During a visit to the United States, she discussed the difficulties of the war and the toll it had taken on the German dogs. The Wagners, whose Mazelaine Kennel was founded on Frau Stockmann's line through Champion Sigurd, the first dog she had ever sold to an American, and his grandsons, Dorian von Marienhof and Utz von Dom, gave her a pick male from one of their top litters. Two years later, that puppy, Czardus of Mazelaine, became a German Champion. She also took two Sirrah Crest dogs, Abra Dabra and Goody Goody, with her on her return to Germany.

It is interesting to note that during this visit to the United States she judged a show in Los Angeles that had a ten-week-old puppy belonging to Dr. and Mrs. Rafael Harris of the Sirrah Crest kennel. She took one look at "Little Lustig," a fawn with a white mask and white paws, and placed him at the head of his class. This puppy, the young Bang Away of Sirrah Crest, went on to become one of the greatest American Champion legends of all time. He set a record for winning more than one hundred Best in Show awards.

The Boxer remains one of Germany's most popular pets. This is Ivette v.d. Boxer-Gilde owned by Brigitie Miller, Germany.

Frau Stockmann returned to Germany with dogs meant to replenish the depleted gene pool of the von Dom bloodline.

However, not long after Czardus's championship, financial problems once again took precedence and he was sold to a man in England, who in turn, sold him to an American officer. Thus, Czardus was the only American Boxer to become a German Champion and then return home to America.

And so it went for Frau Stockmann. Through no fault of her own, her resolve to keep and promote her best dogs often outstripped her ability to do what she really wanted for them. She often sold her best dogs to keep those that were not the most beautiful or the best. It was her champions that saved the rest, time after time. And it was her unwavering dedication that has allowed the rest of us to enjoy this wonderful breed—the Boxer—with all its beauty, personality and abilities.

HISTORY in the United States

The early history of the Boxer in the United States is poorly documented. The well-known, all-rounder judge, Charles G. Hopton, remembered two Boxers being shown at the 1898 Westminster Show, and Frank Bigler reported rumors of Boxers being shown in Chicago in 1904. The first Boxer to finish a championship in the United States was Sgr. Damph von Dom in 1915. He was owned by the New York Governor and Mrs. Herbert G. Lehman. While there were a few Boxer fanciers in the 1920s, it was not until the early 1930s that the breed began to catch on.

Marcia and Jack Fennessy of Cirrol Kennels imported the International Champion Check von Hunnenstein in 1932. He was campaigned extensively and was the first Boxer to win a Best in Show. More importantly, he was a great dog with a marvelous personality that made friends for the breed wherever he went. As there were few quality bitches, Check sired nothing of outstanding merit. However, he did exert a great influence on the breed and his name will be found in the pedigrees of many great dogs through his grandson, Champion Dorian von Marienhof.

Ch. Dorian von Marienhof, a German import, was the first Boxer to win the Working Group at the Westminster Kennel Club Dog Show in 1937.

The first bitch to earn a championship was Dodi von der Stoeckersburg, bred by Henry Stoecker and owned by Mrs. Miriam Breed. That same year, 1933, Birbama Crab became the first American-bred Boxer to place in the Group. Then, in May 1934, Mrs. Miriam Breed purchased the imported champion Sigurd von Dom for her recently established Barmere Kennel.

Sigurd was heavily campaigned and took many Group and Best in Show honors. Called by some "the Father of

the American Boxer," Sigurd was an exceptional fawn dog with an outstanding personality. Thus, 1935 saw a great upswing in the popularity of the Boxer as well as the founding of the American Boxer Club.

At the same time, the American Kennel Club was also growing and maturing. Rules and regulations were being enacted. Breeders were being encouraged to show their American-bred dogs. Parent clubs were being formed and admitted as member clubs under the AKC banner. This occurred for the American Boxer Club in May of 1935. Upon admission, they petitioned to have the Boxer moved from the Non-Sporting Group to the Working Group, which occurred later that year. In addition, 1935 was the first big year for Boxers in the United States. Not only were the numbers steadily increasing but the quality and success of the breed in competition had shown that a good Boxer could stand on its own against other breeds.

Then, in 1936, Mr. and Mrs. John P. Wagner, imported German Champion Dorian von Marienhof for their Mazelaine Kennel. In Germany, Dorian had been declared, almost unanimously, to be outstanding among the greatest show dogs then in existence. His American tour only continued to add to his reputation. After only 21 months in the country, he was shown at a total of 34 shows and remained undefeated in his own breed with an amazing 29 Working Group firsts and 22 Bests in Show. In addition, he was the first Boxer to take a Working Group One at the Westminster show in 1937.

Ch. Bang Away of Sirrah Crest, winner of 121 Best in Show awards, including Westminster Kennel Club, made the Boxer famous in America.

Dorian, who was a Sigurd
grandson on one side and a Check
grandson on the other, left his
mark on the American Boxer
world, not only through his
outstanding show career but, more importantly, through
his get. He was one of the few really great Boxers of the
time to reproduce his quality directly, siring over 35
American-bred champions in a comparatively short time.

Another of the early cornerstones of the American
Boxer world was the International Champion Lustig von
Dom who was imported by Mr. and Mrs. Erwin Freund
for their Tugley Wood Kennel. Arriving in March of 1937,
Lustig finished his championship within one week of his
first show with a Best in Show, two Group firsts and one
Group fourth. Remembering that Lustig was four years
old when he came to the United States, he was shown a
total of 21 times, finishing undefeated in his own breed
with 13 Group firsts and two Bests in Show. One of his
most noted wins was Best of Breed at the 1938

Westminster show under Herr Philip Stockmann. He sired a total of 87 litters in the United States and his impact on the breed is well known.

Another great dog of the 1930s was another Mazelaine import, Utz von Dom. He arrived in the United States in April 1939. Shown a total of 50 times, he was awarded a total of 48 Bests of Breed, 25 Group firsts, 15 Group seconds, three Group thirds and five Group fourths. He won Best in Show a total of four times before his retirement from the show ring in 1940.

It is interesting to note that the first Boxer to place first in the Group at Westminster was Dorian von Marienhof in 1937, the second was Utz von Dom in 1940 and the third was the great Warlord of Mazelaine, an Utz son out of a Dorian daughter. Both Dorian and Utz had been imported by the Wagners of Mazelaine Kennel. Warlord was out of a Mazelaine breeding.

The period from 1946 to 1956 has become known as the "Golden Age of the Boxer." In all areas there was unprecedented growth in the breed. The Boxer began to dominate the dog show ring with multiple Group and Best in Show wins.

Warlord, who began his outstanding career with an American Boxer Club win from the classes, was the first Boxer to take a Best in Show at Westminster. This occurred in 1947. Two years later, Ch. Mazelaine's Zazarac Brandy also won Westminster and set a record of 56 all-breed Best in Show wins. However, Brandy's record was not to endure

Ch. Barrage of Quality Hill won the Working Group at Westminster in 1955 and 1957 and the American Boxer Club National Specialty in 1956.

Ch. Turo's Futurian of Cachet owned by Jeff and Nan Eisley-Bennett winning the Working Group at Westminster in 1996.

for long. Within months, the spectacular Ch. Bang Away of Sirrah Crest came to the forefront.

Owned by Dr. and Mrs. Harris, Bang Away, as an unnamed puppy, had attracted a lot of attention in Los Angeles when he was placed Best in Match by Frau Stockmann. She had called him "Little Lustig" and declared him to be the "best Boxer in America today." Debuting in 1950 at the ABC, he became the third Boxer to win Best in Show at Westminster. He was campaigned extensively in 1952 and broke the record for all-breed Best in Show wins at the Trenton Kennel Club in May of that year.

Bang Away was the most publicized dog of all time. He appeared in *Life*, *Colliers*, *Esquire* and many dog magazines and newspapers. He was recognized and admired by all. Needless to say, he had a major impact on the breed, having sired 81 American champions as well as a number of foreign titlists. Of these, seven became top producers as well, including Ch. Barrage of Quality Hill, another outstanding show dog.

Bang Away made such an impact that he was honored at a dinner held the night before the 1956 ABC Specialty at the Shelton Hotel. This has since become known as the "This Is Your Life Bang Away" testimonial banquet in honor of Ch. Bang Away of Sirrah Crest. His owners were presented with a scrapbook detailing his Best in Show record and champion get. At the proper time, Bang Away was led into the room where he received a standing ovation. For the rest of the evening, Bang Away, himself, presided at the head table resplendent in a rhinestone collar and now-famous crown, being fed bites of fillet by a maitre d' from a Sheffield platter. The tribute to Bang Away fascinated the press and provided even more publicity for the breed and the ABC.

The Golden Age ended somewhere in the mid-1950s, but interest in the Boxer remained strong. The breed continued to dominate the Working Group at Westminster with Ch. Sparkplug taking the honor in 1954; Ch. Barrage of Quality Hill in 1955 and 1957; Ch. Baroque of Quality Hill, a Barrage litter-mate, in 1956; and Ch. Marjack's Golden Windjammer in 1958. Two years later, a Bang Away son, Ch. Marquam Hill's Commanche would win the Group.

In addition to the Boxer's success in the show ring, the period from 1944 to 1955 heralded a major increase in the number of Boxers competing in the obedience ring. There were indeed brains behind that beauty.

Following the Golden Era of the Boxer, there was a slow transition from large kennel operations of 100+ dogs to smaller breeders. However, the Boxer, as a breed, remained strong and continued to produce more than its share of top-winning champions, including Ch. Eldic's Landlord, Ch. Treceder's Painted Lady and the fabulous Salgray "F" litter of six champions: Fashion Plate, Flying High, Flaming Ember, Flame Crest, Fanfare and Frolic, as well as Ch. Millan's Fashion Hint and Ch. Arriba's Prima Donna.

The 1970 Westminster show once again saw a Boxer take the Best in Show win. This time it was the bitch, Ch. Arriba's Prima Donna.

From this point on, the numbers of champion Boxers being produced from a wide range of kennels becomes too numerous to mention. Many of the kennel names are still recognizable from the earlier periods while many have been added throughout the years. Some more recent names you may recognize include TuRo, Jacquet, Cherokee Oaks, Holly Lane, Merrilane, Hi Tech and many, many more.

Today many famous American kennels continue to produce quality champions. This is Ch. Jacquet's Cambridge Fortune bred by the author.

STANDARD for the Boxer

A standard of any breed is the written description of the ideal specimen of that breed. While no dog is perfect, breeders attempt to come as close as possible with each successive generation. The content of the American Kennel Club standard for each recognized breed is controlled by the recognized parent club for that breed. In order to revise a breed standard, the parent club must adhere to certain guidelines set down by the American Kennel Club, propose a revision to the membership of the parent club and wait out an affirmative vote of both the parent club membership and the American Kennel Club.

In the case of the Boxer, the American Boxer Club is the responsible organization. The most recent revision was approved by the American Kennel Club on March 14, 1989. Many think it is a more concise, clear and correct version than the previous standard approved in September 1980.

This revision was undertaken when the American Kennel Club began requiring that all breed standards

The Boxer's well-developed muscles are clean and hard, appearing smooth under taut skin. This is Jacquet's Elsa of Phoenix bred by the author.

conform to a uniform format and guidelines. Thus, the order of the principal elements of the standard was already structured. In addition, the description of each part required condensing and clarifying to eliminate unnecessary and repetitive wording. Only the most serious faults were allowed to be listed.

More recently, the American Kennel Club suggested that the parent club add illustrations to enhance the understanding of the standard. So, in November 1991, the

Although it is common practice in Germany and America to crop a Boxer's ears, this practice is illegal in England, Australia, Holland, and a number of other countries.

This is Ch. Hi-Tech's Arbitrage owned by Dr. and Mrs. William Truesdale.

The Boxer combines strength and agility with elegance and style. This is Ch. Jacquet's Greggson bred by Rick Tomita and Ed Goldfield.

American Boxer Club approved a series of drawings by Eleanor Linderholm Wood. This *Illustrated Standard* booklet is available to the general public.

AKC STANDARD FOR THE BOXER

General Appearance— The *ideal* Boxer is a medium-sized, square built dog of good substance with short back, strong limbs, and short, tight-fitting coat. His well developed muscles are clean, hard and appear smooth under taut skin. His movements denote energy. The gait is firm, yet elastic, the stride free and ground-covering, the carriage proud. Developed to serve as guard, working and companion dog, he combines strength and agility with elegance and style. His expression is alert and temperament steadfast and tractable.

The chiseled head imparts to the Boxer a unique individual stamp. It must be in correct proportion to the body. The broad, blunt muzzle is the distinctive feature, and great value is placed upon its being of proper form and balance with the skull.

In judging the Boxer, first consideration is given to general appearance to which attractive color and arresting style contribute. Next is overall balance with special attention devoted to the head, after which the individual body components are examined for their correct construction, and efficiency of gait is evaluated.

The Boxer's head must be in proportion to the body. The broad, blunt muzzle is the distinctive feature. This is Kimyel Crossfire.

Size, Proportion, Substance— *Height—* Adult males 22 $1/2$ to 25 inches; females 21 to 23 $1/2$ inches at the withers. Preferably, males should not be under the minimum nor females over the maximum; however, proper balance and quality in the individual should be of primary importance since there is no size disqualification. *Proportion—*The body in profile is of square proportion in that a horizontal line from the front of the forechest to the rear projection of the upper thigh should equal the length of a vertical line dropped from the top of the withers to the ground. *Substance—*Sturdy with balanced musculature. Males larger boned than their female counterparts.

Head—The beauty of the head depends upon harmonious proportion of muzzle to skull. The blunt muzzle is $1/3$rd the length of the head from the occiput to the tip of the nose, and $2/3$rds the width of the skull. The head should be clean, not showing deep wrinkles (wet). Wrinkles typically appear upon the forehead when ears are erect, and folds are always present from the lower edge of the stop running downwards on both sides of the muzzle. **Expression**— Intelligent and alert. **Eyes**—Dark brown in color, not too small, too protruding or too deep-set. Their mood-mirroring character combined with the wrinkling of the forehead gives the Boxer head its unique quality of expressiveness. **Ears**—Set at the highest points of the sides of the skull, are cropped, cut rather long and tapering, raised when alert.

The mood-mirroring character of the eyes combined with the wrinkling of the forehead gives the Boxer head its unique expressive quality. Owners, the Heldenbrands.

Skull—The top of the skull is slightly arched, not rounded, flat nor noticeably broad, with the occiput not overly pronounced. The forehead shows a slight indentation between the eyes and forms a distinct stop with the topline of the muzzle. The cheeks should be relatively flat and not bulge (cheekiness), maintaining the clean lines of the skull, and should taper into the muzzle in a slight, graceful curve. **Muzzle**— The muzzle, proportionately developed in length, width and depth, has a shape influenced first through the formation of both jawbones, second through the placement of the teeth, and third through the texture of the lips. The top of the muzzle should not slant down (downfaced), nor should it be concave (dishfaced); however, the tip of the nose should lie slightly higher than the root of the muzzle.

The nose should be broad and black.

The upper jaw is broad where attached to the skull

and maintains this breadth except for a very slight tapering to the front. The lips, which complete the formation of the muzzle, should meet evenly in front. The upper lip is thick and padded, filling out the frontal space created by the projection of the lower jaw, and laterally is supported by the canines of the lower jaw. Therefore, these canines must stand far apart and be of good length so that the front surface of the muzzle is broad and squarish and, when viewed from the side, shows moderate layback. The chin should be perceptible from the side as well as the front. *Bite*—The Boxer bite is undershot; the lower jaw protrudes beyond the upper and curves slightly upward. The incisor teeth of the lower jaw are in a straight line, with the canines preferably up front in the same line to give the jaw the greatest possible width. The upper line of incisors is slightly convex with the corner upper incisors fitting snugly back of the lower canine teeth on each side. *Faults*—Skull too broad. Cheekiness. Wrinkling too deep (wet) or lacking (dry). Excessive flews. Muzzle too light for skull. Too pointed a bite (snipy), too undershot, teeth or tongue showing when mouth closed. Eyes noticeably lighter than ground color of coat.

Neck, Topline, Body— *Neck*—Round, of ample length, muscular and clean without excessive, hanging skin (dewlap). The neck has a distinctly marked nape with an elegant arch blending smoothly into the withers. *Topline*—Smooth, firm and slightly sloping. *Body*—The chest is of fair width, and the forechest well defined and visible from the side. The brisket is deep, reaching down to the elbows; the depth of the body at the lowest part of the brisket equals half the height of the dog at the withers. The ribs extending far to the rear, are well arched but not barrel-shaped. The back is short, straight and muscular, and firmly connects the withers to the hindquarters. The loins are short and muscular. The lower stomach line is slightly tucked up, blending into a graceful curve to the rear. The croup is slightly sloped, flat and broad. *Faults*–Short, heavy neck. Chest too broad, too narrow or hanging between shoulders. Lack of forechest. Hanging stomach. Slab-sided rib cage. Long or narrow loin, weak union with croup. Falling off of croup. Higher in rear than in front.

Forequarters—The shoulders are long and sloping, close-lying, and not excessively covered with muscle (loaded). The upper arm is long, approaching a right angle to the shoulder blade. The elbows should not press too closely to the chest wall nor stand off visibly from it. The forelegs are long, straight and firmly muscled and when viewed from the front, stand parallel to each other. The pastern is strong and distinct, slightly slanting, but standing almost perpendicular to the ground. The dewclaws may be removed. Feet should be compact, turning neither in nor out, with well arched toes. *Faults*—Loose or loaded shoulders. Tied in or bowed out elbows.

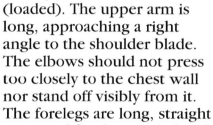

The Boxer's forelegs stand parallel to each other. The hindquarters are strongly muscled with angulation in balance with that of the forequarters. Owners, Sam and Win Bitler.

Hindquarters—The hindquarters are strongly muscled with angulation in balance with that of the forequarters. The thighs are broad and curved, the breech musculature hard and strongly developed. Upper and lower thigh long. Leg well angulated at the stifle with a clearly defined, well "let down" hock joint. Viewed from behind, the hind legs should be straight with hock joints leaning neither in nor out.

From the side, the leg below the hock (metatarsus) should be almost perpendicular to the ground, with a slight slope to the rear permissible. The metatarsus should be short, clean and strong. The Boxer has no rear dewclaws. *Faults*—Steep or over-angulated hindquarters. Light thighs or underdeveloped hams. Over-angulated (sickle) hocks. Hindquarters too far under or too far behind.

In the Boxer fawn shades vary from light tan to mahogany. Breeder, Rick Tomita.

Coat—Short, shiny, lying smooth and tight to the body.

Color—The colors are fawn and brindle. Fawn shades vary from light tan to mahogany. The brindle ranges from sparse, but clearly defined black stripes on a fawn background, to such a heavy concentration of black striping that the essential fawn background color barely, although clearly shows through (which may give the appearance of "reverse brindling"). White markings should be of such distribution as to enhance the dog's appearance, but may not exceed one-third of the entire coat. They are not desirable on the flanks or on the back of the torso proper. On the face, white may replace part of the otherwise essential black mask and may extend in an upward path between the eyes, but it must not be excessive, so as to detract from true Boxer expression. *Faults*—Unattractive or misplaced white markings. *Disqualifications*—Boxers that are any color other than fawn or brindle. Boxers with a total of white markings exceeding one-third of the entire coat.

The brindle coat is made up of clearly defined black stripes on a fawn background. Breeder, Rick Tomita.

Gait—Viewed from the side, proper front and rear angulation is manifested in a smoothly efficient, level-backed, ground covering stride with powerful drive emanating from a freely operating rear. Although the front legs do not contribute impelling power, adequate "reach" should be evident to prevent interference, overlap or "sidewinding" (crabbing). Viewed from the front, the shoulders should remain trim and the elbows not flare out. The legs are parallel until gaiting narrows the track in proportion to increasing speed, then the legs come in under the body but should never cross. The line from the shoulder down through the leg should remain straight although not necessarily perpendicular to the ground. Viewed from the rear, a Boxer's rump should not roll. The hind feet should "dig in" and track relatively true with the front. Again, as speed increases, the normally broad rear track will become narrower. *Faults*—Stilted or inefficient gait. Lack of smoothness.

Character and Temperament—These are of paramount importance in the Boxer. Instinctively a "hearing" guard dog, his hearing is alert, dignified and self-assured. In the show ring, his behavior should exhibit constrained animation. With family and friends, his temperament is fundamentally playful, yet patient and stoical with children. Deliberate and wary with strangers, he will exhibit curiosity but, most importantly, fearless courage if threatened. However, he responds promptly to friendly overtures honestly rendered. His intelligence, loyal affection and tractability to discipline make him a highly desirable companion. *Faults*—Lack of dignity and alertness. Shyness.

DISQUALIFICATIONS

Boxers that are any color other than fawn or brindle. Boxers with

White Boxers or Boxers with white markings exceeding one-third of the coat are undesirable.

a total of white markings exceeding one-third of the entire coat.

INTERPRETING THE STANDARD
by Drs. Daniel and Jean Buchwald

As previously mentioned, the breed standard describes the ideal specimen of the breed. However, since no dog is perfect, it is the comprehensive understanding and constant comparison of individual dogs to the ideal that are important. It is an educational process that will ultimately provide a sound foundation for additional breed knowledge acquired over the years.

Initially, a person new to the Boxer breed should read the standard thoroughly to achieve a general idea of what to look for in the dog he wishes to obtain. While it will still be necessary to rely heavily on the chosen breeder's more extensive knowledge, it will at least alert you to what is not desirable in a given dog.

The Boxer responds promptly to friendly overtures, such as a hug from a friend. This is Andrew De Prisco with a Boxer bred by the author.

Before embarking on an overview of the Boxer standard, there are four concepts that apply to all dogs:

1. TYPE: Type is defined as the group of features that a dog must have in order to be a representative of its breed. These features are usually contained in the General Appearance section of the standard.

2. STYLE: Style refers to the elegance and carriage of the dog. A stylish dog will possess those subtle extra details that give him a noble air.

3. SOUNDNESS: A sound dog is one that is correctly built with a healthy mind and body. In a working breed, a sound dog is one that is physically and mentally fit to perform the work for which it was bred, like an athlete ready to compete.

4. QUALITY: Quality is the sum of the desired structural features a dog possesses. The closer a dog comes to the ideal specimen, the higher the quality of the dog.

General Appearance

The standard calls for a squarely built animal. Good length of leg and short loins are necessary to a square dog. This squareness results in a better general appearance and a movement that is more efficient.

Substance

The standard differentiates the aspects of masculinity and femininity. These are the features that give the male a masculine look and the female a feminine look. Clear sexual definition is expected in the Boxer. Thus, the female should be somewhat smaller and lighter than the male.

Boxers should not show teeth or tongue when the mouth is closed. Boxer bred by the author.

Head

Since the chiseled head imparts to the Boxer a unique individual stamp, special attention should be paid to its requirements.

The proportion of the muzzle to the skull is probably its most distinctive feature. A strong, deep and wide muzzle is the desired result of well-formed jaws with correctly placed teeth and well-cushioned lips.

Proper proportion among the parts of the head, along with proper eye color, shape and placement, and alertness create the true Boxer expression. Owner, Siegi Lehman.

The relation between the upper and lower jaw structure produces an undershot bite, that is, the lower incisors are placed forward of the upper ones.

Boxers should not show teeth or tongue when the mouth is closed. If this happens, not only is the bite in some way incorrect, usually excessively undershot, but the desired expression will be ruined.

The proper proportion among the parts of the head, along with proper eye color, shape and placement, when alert will create the true Boxer expression. As a general principle, bad heads do not produce correct expressions. If the expression is off, something else about the head is also off.

The neck should be of ample length, muscular and elegantly arched. It is especially enhanced by an alert carriage. This is Walkon Wotta Smasha of Walkon Boxers, Scotland.

Neck

The desired neck is of ample length, muscular and elegantly arched. This feature is especially enhanced by an alert carriage.

Body

Square with a short, straight and muscular back that firmly connects the front and rear assemblies.

Front Angulation

The proper placement of the scapula and humerus is directly related to the arching of the ribs. These bones lay over the ribs in such a manner that flat ribs tend to cause steeper angulation. Ribs that are too rounded or barrel shaped will restrict the frontal movement and spread the front legs further apart in a bulldog-like appearance.

Good front angulation will affect a number of important aspects of the dog. It will provide for a smooth neck insertion, evidence good frontal

With regard to the forequarters, strong bones and compact feet are desired in the Boxer. This is AmCan. Ch. Fiero's Tally Ho Tailo bred by Ingrid Feder and co-owned with Dr. & Mrs. Truesdale.

projection of the forechest and allow the elbows to set level with a chest of good depth which prevents the elbows from turning under the dog's body. Proper angulation will also impart good reach to the front assembly. Dogs that can take a longer step will cover more ground with less effort than those that are restricted to shorter steps.

Strong bones and compact feet are also desired in the Boxer.

Hindquarters

The rear angulation must be equal or very close to

that of the front. A balanced front and rear are the keys to proper movement.

Gait

Gait, or movement, is closely related to angulation. The efficiency of the gait is a result of well-coordinated and ample steps. If the front and rear angulation are out of balance with each other, smooth coordination is lost.

Color

The color of the Boxer's coat enhances his overall beauty. Both fawn and brindle are equally accepted colors. The black mask is a must for the Boxer. It covers the muzzle and gradually blends into the ground color as it reaches the border of the muzzle/skull transition. Darker shadings around the eyes are always present. White markings on the face, when present, will naturally cover the black mask to some extent.

White markings, while not essential, are usually welcome as long as they enhance the appearance of the dog.

They should not exceed one-third of the entire coat and are not desirable on the flanks or the back of the torso.

Brindling is usually when black striping is distinctly striated in herring-bone pattern over the fawn background.

Character and Temperament

These are of paramount importance in the Boxer. Boxers should be alert, dignified and self-assured in bearing with somewhat constrained animation in the show ring. However, with family and friends they are fundamentally playful, yet patient with children. They exhibit a sheer joy of life that is unequalled in most other breeds.

Boxers are playful yet patient with children. This is Adam Koester with Seneca.

White markings, while not essential, are welcome as long as they enhance the appearance of the Boxer and do not exceed one-third of the coat. Owner, Carol Beusee.

ROLES of Today's Boxer

T he calm, steady temperament and outgoing personality of the Boxer are ideal for therapy work. The breed has an almost uncanny ability to adjust to almost any situation. They are able to sense the needs of each individual with whom they come in contact and modify their behavior accordingly. One minute the dog may be playing energetically with a boisterous child and the next minute sitting quietly while being petted by an elderly wheelchair-bound individual.

Bosco owned by the Michals family started doing therapy work at the age of three months at Neptune Conva Center in New Jersey. Breeder, Rick Tomita.

However, those interested in therapy work should understand that there is more to the program than the innate instincts of the Boxer.

While they make ideal candidates, there is a degree of training involved. Depending upon the maturity and self-confidence of an older puppy, nine to12 months of age, they can be introduced to the therapeutic setting. These may include hospital wards, institutional living situations, special education classes as well as senior-citizen facilities. The ideal situation is to have an older, more experienced dog along to help

Bosco and Spiros Michals visit with a resident. Owners of therapy dogs derive a sense of satisfaction from contributing to the community as well as bonding with their dogs.

with the training. In all cases, the owner/handler needs to keep a close eye on the trainee to monitor behavior and reactions to a variety of stimuli as well as safety. Some facilities will require that the dog be certified as a therapy dog before being allowed to visit, while others will permit younger trainees to participate.

There are numerous benefits arising from participation in therapy dog activities. The owner/ handler derives a sense of satisfaction from contributing to the community as well as a closer working relationship with their dog. The dogs develop unique relationships with the people they meet as they mature in their emotional and mental capacities as well as acting as goodwill ambassadors for the breed. Perhaps best of all are the reactions of those that are being visited. This may be their only opportunity to interact with another living creature, especially one that extends unconditional friendship regardless of the circumstances.

One organization, Therapy Dogs International, uses the AKC Good Citizenship test together with exposure to specialized equipment to qualify the dogs for certification. Those who succeed are the ones with good, stable temperaments and responsiveness to gently given commands.

To date, there are approximately 100 Boxers registered with Therapy Dogs International in the United States and Canada.

Bosco waits at the top of the practice stairs, which are used to help senior citizens practice successfully going up and down stairs.

GUIDE DOGS

The German Shepherd Dog was the first breed to be trained as guide dogs for the blind and continue to serve admirably in that capacity. However, Boxers, too, can function as loyal and trustworthy guide dogs. They are friendly dogs with a small frame yet a strong pull.

One graduate who will use only Boxers says, "They are proud of their work. They travel well and are not afraid of anything. They are willing to please when in harness, but playful when not at work. They are observant and aware of everything."

Casey, with her trainer/ handler Lea Bowling, graduating at the top of her class from Seeing Eye.™

Seeing Eye™ Boxers undergo the same training as any other breed. They begin in volunteer puppy homes where they learn basic obedience and become exposed to a variety of situations they may encounter in their working capacity. When the pup is about 14 months old, he returns to the Seeing Eye™ facility to begin his formal training for guide work. For three months he is taught to guide along progressively more difficult routes and to navigate heavy pedestrian and vehicular traffic. Following the successful completion of training, the dog is matched with a person. The new team then trains for an additional three to four weeks under the supervision of an instructor.

Since its founding in 1929, the Seeing Eye™ Foundation has matched over 10,000 specially bred and trained guide dogs with people throughout the United States and Canada.

CHOOSING a Boxer Puppy

A female or a male? A bitch is smaller than a male, if space is a factor. Do you live in a condo/apartment, a cottage, a small house? If you are a small person, light in weight, you might find a bitch easier to manage on a leash and collar. A bitch is unlikely to roam or stray from home; however, when in season and having been bred before, she may run off to look for a mate.

I have found a bitch easier to housebreak than a male. She will not likely mark in your house and other indoor areas. However, she'll mark outdoors, even raising her leg similar to a male. This is especially true if she is an alpha bitch or while in season. Unless you designate a spot for her in your yard or use ex pens, your bitch could ruin a beautiful green lawn with brown burn spots. Males in turn lift their leg, usually starting at nine months, and can urinate on and burn expensive ornamental shrubs or ruin furniture and rugs indoors. It is quite easy to teach your Boxer to relieve itself in certain locations starting at an early age. Take the puppy to the spot, perhaps behind a shed, behind trees or bushes, where the grass is not so

Boxer puppies, no matter which sex, should be taught at an early age where to relieve themselves so as not to ruin any of your ornamental shrubs or flowers. Owner, Les Baker.

important or have an area where the ornamental shrubs are not the tender or expensive ones. I take soiled newspaper that has the smell of the pup's urine and/or fecal matter and put it on the spot using a few stones to hold it down. Puppies and dogs usually sniff first, seeming to seek a spot where another dog has gone to urinate and defecate. Notice during housebreaking how the puppy usually will go on the same spot he has made an accident on or anywhere a predecessor has gone.

Two Boxers will enjoy having each other to play with and you can get in on the fun too! Owners, Steven and Ann Anderson.

There are various good odor eliminators available. I especially like the enzymatic ones. They are usually safer and eliminate the odor. There are sprays that stimulate the essence of the herb rue that cuts off the sense of smell when the dog sniffs it, thus turning him

A seven-week-old litter of Boxers bred by Laura Miller of Artistry Boxers.

Male Boxers tend to get along well with canine members of the same sex. This is Logan with his Argentine Dogo buddy, Hunter. Owner, Janine Thorpe.

away from that area. In the wild, wolves, foxes and wild dogs will avoid areas where this herb grows. As we know, the sense of smell is the keenest sense in a canine.

Getting back to the bitch, the cost of spaying a bitch is more expensive than castrating a male dog. In dog shows, I have found the bitch competition tougher since there are more good bitches than dogs. However, more breeders tend to want to hang onto their best bitch or bitches to continue their line; thus, a good quality bitch is more expensive and harder to find than a good quality male.

Something a good breeder will tell you is that it's better to buy a bitch puppy over a male for show. If the pup does not grow into a top show dog, a male ends up being just a good pet, oftentimes not suitable for breeding. However, if a bitch does not turn out and has a good pedigree with no glaring faults, you can always go to a dominant top-producing champion male and perhaps produce your own future show dog. In addition, most conscientious breeders will not breed a non-titled male unless he has considerable attributes to offer.

Another factor to consider when choosing which gender is whether or not you have another dog. I find a male and a female rarely, if ever, get into fights. They may have short quarrels or spats but not the basic fight to the death that some bitches can get into. We are never sure what triggers this behavior but most often the less-alpha bitch decides she wants the alpha position. Unless you are in full control and an alpha figure yourself, it is a difficult problem to solve. However, I have seen and lived with two or even three bitches coexisting for their entire lives with just minor quarrels.

If you decide to get a female Boxer you must think about having her spayed...or the great responsibility of having a litter.

It is very difficult to keep a male and female apart when your female comes in season unless they are kept in different parts of the house with strong gates and closed doors. Children especially find it difficult to keep doors closed. A good solution is to use your dog crate. Without careful planning and control, it is virtually impossible to keep them apart during the heat cycle and not have them breed. Dogs are so instinctive that even males and females that have never bred will get together. Another solution is to board one of your dogs during the heat cycle, with your breeder or at a good, secure kennel. Also, consider the gender of your neighbor's dog, especially if their dog has access to your property, and any dogs that make frequent visits to your home.

Author Rick Tomita with two of his Boxer puppies. Good breeders will be able to help answer your questions when deciding on a puppy.

If your home and yard is roomy enough, I do encourage the new owner never to have an only dog. Get two, preferably a male or female or two females. It is usually better to take one puppy first and have that puppy trained and established in your household, then go purchase the second one. What is nice is that they have each other to play with, to occupy themselves, to exercise and work off their abundance of energy so that they are calmer and make better house pets. I find this practice especially helpful in keeping the show Boxer in optimum condition. Boxers play a game only seen in Boxers. They romp, roll and wrestle utilizing muscles not used in the usual running or jogging. They can be lying down, playing with their necks craning and their mouths open in mock biting, a sort of jousting while they make a cooing sound as if talking among themselves. I can watch these antics for hours.

Males are larger with bigger bone. However, many people think a big male is less manageable. Though, if you properly train your male while he is young and during his maturation, he will be very responsive and you can have complete control.

In most breeds of dogs, bitches are considered the more docile and affectionate to their owners and family. Also, bitches are thought to be gentler with children. I have found, and many Boxer owners will agree, that Boxer males are just as docile to their owners, gentle with children and loving to all members of their household. I have found that the males are a little more loyal and less flighty. I find their affection warmer in feeling. Until you own a male, you will not understand these subtleties. I usually have two or three Boxers living in the house, a male and two females. My entire backyard is fenced and the dogs have access to it from the kitchen door. When they want to go out, they run to the back door. I had one male that watched how I opened the door by turning the knob and then the storm door, which was a latch type. He learned to open both and let himself and the bitches out to relieve themselves. Later he would open the doors and hold them open for the girls. Another time before I padlocked the back gate leading to the driveway, I heard rapping on the back door accompanied by incessant barking. It was my male. I looked for the girls, who were not in the backyard. I asked him where they had gone using their names. He ran to the open gate to show me where they had escaped, not running out himself. I, of course, gave him high praises and hugs and then ran for the girls. This made me love this dog all the more. Every male I have owned has not run off while every bitch I have lived with has taken off at one time or another.

Keeping a Male and a Female Apart

Having both a male and female imposes a responsibility on the owner during the bitch's heat period unless your plan is to breed the two.

You must make provisions to keep them separated during this period. You are generally safe during the first five to seven days, however, so many of the house bitches are so clean that you may not spot the beginning of their cycles. I tell owners of the bitches to watch for any swelling or excessive cleaning/licking of the vaginal area. When they see this, they should dab the vulva with a white tissue or paper towel daily, watching for a reddish color. Count from the first day they see any color.

Separate them from the seventh day on. Although I have seen bitches reach their ovulation in the seventh, eighth and ninth day, this usually occurs in their 12th to 15th day. A bitch should not be bred at too young an age. Some Boxer males are precocious and can breed from six months onward. How fertile they are is another matter. There are many reports of Boxer males being fertile as young as eight months old.

When choosing the sex of a new puppy, children are a consideration. Although females are thought to be gentler with children, Boxer males can be just as docile and gentle.

People tell me, "oh, we watch them," but often when the owners are distracted, for even a moment, an accidental breeding can occur. I remember a breeder friend who housed the male and female in crates next to each other and he told me there was absolutely no way they got together. However, the bitch was quite pregnant and produced five beautiful Boxer pups 63 days from the day they were crated next to each other. Most recently, a young couple asked me to look at their bitch who had a litter ten months ago and again was looking pregnant. Could this be possible? I asked them where they had kept their male puppy that also lives with them. They were separated during the day when they couldn't keep watch, but at night they both slept with them in bed. Besides, the pup couldn't possibly breed his mother. They would certainly know if anything happened in their bed. I asked them what happens when they get off their bed at night? If you suspect that an unwanted breeding has occurred, I urge you to go to the vet for help. These mismate shots can be risky, sometimes causing infections in the uterus, even pyometra. However, these days, there are excellent antibiotics that can alleviate these problems. There are too many unwanted puppies in the world dying for homes. Why bring anymore into the world?

BEFORE YOU BUY

Don't bring a puppy home for the holidays. Don't buy a puppy as a surprise for your wife or husband. Remember that the lady of the house usually ends up taking care of

Although it may seem like a perfect time, don't bring a Boxer puppy home during the holidays. Wait until a less hectic time of year.

Children should always be involved in the selection of a new puppy. Jessica Starr and Michael Harms have made their choice.

the pup and probably does not need the extra work or responsibility. The husband usually has a certain puppy or dog in mind and you cannot pick that dog for him. Do not expect your children, who promised they would take responsibility for the care of the animal, to follow through over the long term. I had an experience where the husband came with two children, lovely people, insisting the wife would be absolutely delighted with a Boxer puppy as her birthday present. After much persistence, they purchased the pup and went home. Two hours later they all returned. They were thrown out of the house. The Mrs. did not appreciate her surprise.

Don't bring a puppy into your home just as you are moving or immediately after a move while you are settling in and getting used to a new environment. Prepare your home for the puppy just the same as if a new baby were coming home. You and your new pup do not need the extra stress.

Don't buy a puppy if a new baby is expected. It takes time and care, at least a year, for the puppy to be brought up properly. The arrival of a new human baby is a big responsibility in itself.

Don't bring a puppy in when you have made plans for a long trip or vacation. A young puppy does not do well in most commercial boarding kennels. Puppies need three feedings a day as well as the weekly ear care. It will also interrupt the bonding process. In addition, immunization is usually incomplete and exposing him to a kennel situation where many dogs congregate is dangerous to the puppy's health. Many responsible breeders will not sell you a puppy if they know any of this will happen. They will tell you to wait. They will also make arrangements with you to hold the puppy until you return or will take in the puppy at a nominal boarding fee for the duration of your trip. Going back to the breeder can be like visiting grandparents. It just amazes me how a Boxer puppy, having been gone, sometimes for years, will remember the breeder. What a fuss they will make. What a happy greeting!

Wild dogs, in their natural habitats, are testing, biting and chewing as they're growing up. Young dogs are always curious and love to learn. That's one of the

Boxer puppies will chew, especially during the ages of six to twelve months. Put things out of harm's way that you don't want chewed or played with.

reasons they chew, especially in the six-to-12-month stage when they are going through their hormonal changes and are sexually maturating. They are doing what nature dictates. They are not being bad. Try being extra understanding and patient. Put things out of harm's way or use helpers, such as Bitter Apple, on things you don't want chewed or played with. Use a spray that will deter the puppy not to

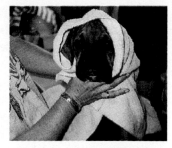

The first bath. Make all your new Boxer puppy's first experiences pleasureable. Owner, Patti Ann Rutledge.

come into the area you wish to make taboo, like your couch or Oriental carpeting.

When you can't attend to your puppy, put him in a crate just as you would a child in a playpen, with chew toys such as Roar-Hide™ or Nylabone®. Keep him out of harm's way and keep him away from your valuables. Having to discipline your puppy constantly can have a negative effect on your puppy as well as yourself. Use these helpers from the time you bring your pup home, especially the crate.

As a first collar, do not start off with a choker, which can be a frightening experience. Use a buckle collar. Initially, put it on for a short while and then begin leaving it on for longer periods of time as he grows. I use a light-weight lead with a small bolt. The puppy will scratch at it because it's a new feeling on his neck. Sometimes, while walking they scratch at it with a hind leg and do a "crab walk," as described by one new owner. She insisted I sold her a defective dog with a problem in his hindquarters and insisted on reimbursement of her money. Her veterinarian also thought there was a problem and insisted on an x-ray. Of course, they found nothing in the x-ray and the puppy got used to the collar and stopped the crab action.

LOCATING A BOXER PUPPY

Having decided on breed, gender and timing, now you begin the painstaking process of finding and selecting the puppy.

In seeking and choosing the puppy, keep these criteria in mind: a great temperament, good structure and soundness (a pleasing balance of both combined with a typey head, robustness, good health and, of course, a good pedigree).

Australian breeder Rosina Olifent-Brace of Sjecoin Kennels holds up two eight-week-old Boxer pups.

Look for advertisements or photographs in various publications such as *Boxer Review*, *Boxer Quarterly* (breed-specific magazines) or high-quality canine publications (*Dogs USA*, *Dog Fancy*, etc.) devoted to multiple breeds. These will list breeders that may be in your area. Then visit the premises where the puppies are born and reared to study their action, their parents and grandparents, if possible. I've always maintained that the puppy you choose reflects its grandparents structurally and temperamentally.

Another good resource is your veterinarian. He might have a breeder or breeders as clients. Also, your vet will usually have a listing of qualified and conscientious breeders in the area in which he practices. Friends or acquaintances who own a

Boxer can often refer you to the breeder they acquired their Boxer from; but only if their dog is a good one. Aim for the

When looking for a Boxer puppy, you should observe the littermates' interaction with one another. Owners, Hope and Barry Blazer.

highest quality possible—the healthiest, the soundest and the best personality. When you have found the right breeder, make an appointment and visit to evaluate the puppies. See which one is active; which one is quiet; which one is more "people" oriented; and, finally, which one connects with you. Presuming the puppy is to live with you for its lifetime, choose the temperament which is most compatible with your personality and lifestyle. Like all relationships, there needs to be compatibility so that a strong bond can occur.

Look for very specific structure. Begin with the overall balance, then look at the head. Boxers are a "head breed." The overall impression should be pleasing to your eye. The muzzle should be broad and have depth. A bump above his nose is a good sign as well as a predictor of a good stop. A high occiput assures good high ear set, giving that alert look. I like to see some wrinkles, a reasonable amount, as some of this disappears

Puppies learn from their dam and littermates and should stay with them until at least eight weeks of age.

as the head grows and matures. I avoid an excess amount of wrinkling, which can give a wet look and is not desirable. Looking down on the pup, pull back the ears into the palm of your hand, the head should resemble a bunny rabbit with fat cheeks. This was pointed out to me by Gerald Broadt, a well-known handler, breeder and AKC judge. Those pups with the bunny look turn out to have the best heads when they mature with width of muzzle, clean cheeks and a narrow skull.

Straight topline and a high tailset together with well angulated hindquarters, a short back and sloping shoulders are desired. If you plan on showing the deep red fawn or brindle color, well pigmented on the head and down the back is most preferred. White markings up the legs and on the chest with a white blaze between the eyes is eye-catching to the judges. White, half or full, collars are a matter of taste. I

An adorable Boxer puppy is hard to resist.

prefer a solid-colored neck which, to my eyes, gives the neck a longer look.

With the bite I like to see the bottom jawline as wide as possible. This usually indicates a nice, straight, wide bottom jaw when the adult teeth come in. I also like to see the jawline as close to the top row of teeth as possible and yet must be undershot. I found that when the second set of teeth comes in, the jawline comes forward. You should not see the tongue when the jaw is closed.

The eyes should be as dark as possible. Puppies have bluish eyes which darken as they age. I have often seen pups with light eyes that do darken with age. Dark haws, the third membrane which adds to a pleasing expression, are preferred. However, I never reject a puppy having one or both haws that are white. That is the least worry regarding the overall quality of the pup. There are other physical concerns, such as poor hindquarters, roachy topline, poor feet, poor temperament, etc., which are more of a distraction and undesired. I do like to see a black muzzle, not brown. Even though there are white markings on the head, the black on the muzzle should be framed around the white. I don't like to see the black extend way over the eyes, which gives a somber look.

The nose should be broad and pigmented or nearly so by six to ten weeks of age. A narrow nose usually indicates a narrow muzzle on maturation, giving a snipey look.

I like to see a pronounced arch in the neck as well as well-angulated hindquarters. This gives the puppy a flowing line from the head to the rear hocks. I've found that what appears to be a lot of angulation does modify. Puppies seem to lose some angulation as they mature. The tail set should be straight out of the back with the tail carried high.

My advice is to seek a good, reputable breeder that has been doing this for some time. Someone who knows his or her lines several generations back as well as other lines that they have incorporated in their breeding and why they did so. Depend on them.

When you visit a breeder to see a litter of pups, take along someone who has dog sense and/or an eye for dogs. Meet owners of dogs that were acquired from this breeder and question them about integrity, their satisfaction (not only for having acquired a good dog but for getting help having questions answered) and for having a nice pleasant relationship with this particular breeder. I treasure the relationship and memories of the breeder and all the people who were helpful to me when I first acquired my Boxers 25 years ago. I am still on friendly terms with them. They are my teachers and are like a part of my family.

When you do find a puppy that has caught your eye and heart, it may be expensive, especially if it is a show or breeding quality. My motto has been, "you pay for what you get." Most good and reputable breeders don't spare expense for food, supplements, veterinary care, housing, proper heat in winter, proper exercise and perhaps even proper socialization by hiring good sitters or kennel help. Consider all this when purchasing a puppy.

Jack-in-the-Boxers...Choosing a Boxer puppy should not be a quick decision, rather it should take time and careful preparation.

A good breeder will want you to take over where he left off. A good breeder will have taught the puppy the first steps toward housebreaking and perhaps leash training.

EVERYDAY CARE of the Puppy

Before bringing your new puppy home, or as you bring him into the house, provide a crate. A crate not only will help in the housebreaking but will provide the puppy with a place of its own, a place where it will feel secure. In the beginning, you might want to shred newspaper and put it in the crate. Once the puppy is housebroken, the crate will become invaluable to you especially if you work outside the home and the puppy will be alone much of the day. As you know, the puppy will go through a chewing stage. If he is not crated, he will chew anything and everything. By crating, you will be

A crate will help in housebreaking. In the beginning you might want to shred some newspaper and put it in the crate.

protecting your home and your puppy from chewing something that could be dangerous, like wires, plants, and small objects that could get caught in his throat. Leave a couple of Nylabones® and/or Roar-Hide™ in the crate with the puppy. When you come home and let him out of the crate to relieve himself, praise him. Eventually, you will be able to leave him loose in the house while you are gone but leave the crate door open and don't be surprised if you find him sleeping in the crate. It is important to remember that the crate should *not* be used as punishment when the puppy does something wrong. You don't want the puppy to

The crate you buy should be big enough to accommodate your Boxer as an adult. Note the general cage divider used to reduce the size of the crate according to size of pup to aid in housebreaking.

associate the crate with being punished. When you put him in the crate, give him a treat and praise him. As he grows, he will still use the crate because it is the place where he feels safe and secure.

Bringing up Babies

When the pups all eat together in a litter, competition stimulates the appetite. When a puppy goes off with a family and is on its own, it has been frequently known not to eat as well or, in some cases, not to eat at all. Following is the feeding instructions I give to all puppy owners:

"A good basic meal would consist of dry food, about ³/₄ cup of fresh hamburger cooked in about ¹/₂ cup water, ¹/₂ cup to ³/₄ cup cottage cheese. Vitamin C is the most important supplement and should be added once a day. Additional items that can be added are: boiled rice and barley, cooked egg yolks for puppies (no raw whites), cooked whole eggs for adults, wheat germ, beef stew with vegetables, chicken stew with vegetables, most cooked vegetables—carrots, tomatoes, celery. For liquid you can use: meat juices, broth, or soup. Canned dog food can be added to the dry food to encourage a fussy eater."

During this phase, supplement the pup with a high-calorie appetite stimulator that will keep him nourished and prevent too much weight loss. It is said, don't fuss too much and the puppy will eat when it gets hungry enough. I have difficulty with this since some pups

When puppies eat together in a litter, competition stimulates the appetite and the need to feed.

do go into slight depressions when taken away from littermates—"separation anxiety." I think coaxing is a part of the bonding process between you and your new pup. Once you have the puppy eating, then less fussing is needed. Only in a few isolated cases have we produced a fussy eater in later life and this can be a nightmare. Eat! Eat! Please eat!

Vitamins could be added. An all-natural vitamin with fatty acids is an excellent choice that can be added to a meal. Other useful vitamins are vitamin E, vitamin C, wheat germ oil, a combination of oils and elemental sulfur (helpful for fleas), Brewer's yeast and garlic seem helpful with fleas as well as being beneficial and appetizing. Bones should be limited to Nylabones®, Gumabones®, and Roar-Hide™.

Natural bones can be brittle and stick in the throat and injure organ linings. The Nylabones®, Gumabones®, and Roar-Hide™ help to keep the teeth clean and strong.

If a puppy or adult won't eat, entice it with canned cat food. Dogs love the smell and the taste. They also love to eat cat droppings so use cat litter pans that have covers or put the box in an area where your Boxer cannot access it.

Gumabones® are better for puppies due to their softer composition. Puppy bred by the author.

Some puppies are known to eat their own stools. I laughingly refer to this as recycling. However, it is not healthy for the pup nor pleasant to have the puppy give you a lick after he has eaten his own stool. There are remedies that have been successful. Monosodium glutamate sprinkled on the puppy's food, powdered seaweed or kelp in pellets or tablets has worked or try an enzymatic acting supplement. When these are digested, they break down the appeal of the stool, making it unappetizing for the pups. Better yet, pick up immediately after each bowel movement and dispose.

During the first week away from the littermates, the puppy will be lonely. They are used to having companions. At night I suggest placing the pup in a dog crate with an artificial lambskin for warmth. The wool will feel like a littermate. You can also set the crate up in your bedroom or a child's bedroom near the bed so the puppy can feel human presence. There are wooly toys with squeakers in them that are quite tough for the pups to play with and snuggle up to. If the pup cries in the night, reassure him by softly talking to him while putting your hand or finger into the crate. This will reassure him that he is not alone. This might go on for a few nights. Be patient and understanding. Don't rattle the crate or frighten him. You want him to feel comfortable and happy in his crate, which is his bedroom, his space, his den and just generally a secure place. The collapsible-type crates are ideal for moving in and out of the bedroom.

When you awaken in the morning, take the puppy out immediately. Wait until the pup makes its bowel movement before bringing him in. They invariably seem to have to do this. If you don't, the pup will make the second load, so to speak, in the house. During the day, take the puppy out after every nap and, of course, after every meal. In the winter, many

breeders will have paper-trained them, although Boxer pups seem to train themselves on paper. Put the newspaper in front of

An artificial lambskin will help to keep a puppy warm; the wool will feel like a littermate. Puppy bred by the author.

A collapsible crate is ideal for moving in and out of the bedroom.

the door you will be using to take the pup out, usually the back door that leads to your backyard. I recommend a fenced-in yard or a fenced run area or exercise pen. You know then that the puppy is in a safe area and cannot wander off and get lost, stolen or hit by a car. If you do not have a fenced yard, always walk the puppy on a leash. Never allow your puppy to walk over the threshold of your house without a leash and collar. If you get in the habit of doing this each and every time, the puppy, as it grows, will not have the tendency to dash out the door ahead of you. Many dear pets have been killed or maimed by running into the path of an oncoming vehicle.

I've also found that when Boxers, being loyal companions, are not allowed to wander off the property, on or off leash, until at least a year of age, there is a tendency for the adult not to leave the property. If your puppy does run away, don't chase

If your Boxer puppy runs away from you, don't chase after him. Try running in the opposite direction toward the house and away from danger. Puppy bred by the author.

him. He will think it is a game and he will usually continue to run away from you. Try running in the opposite direction, away from danger or toward your home, calling him vigorously and enthusiastically, "Buster, come." If this doesn't work, drop to the ground on your knees or completely down and pretend to cry. If you have created a bond, the puppy will usually come to see that you are all right as long as he is not distracted or chasing something.

I teach my puppies through the Alpha concept, by becoming the mother or father of the puppy, praising with enthusiasm and gusto in a happy-sounding voice. If you have to discipline your puppy, use a voice that is grave, with the sound of a growl. The puppy will remember this from the time he lived with his dam. There are several excellent books that go into great detail on this concept. Never strike your puppy with your hand, a rolled-up newspaper, etc. If you must get physical, grab the scruff of the neck gently or use a collar and leash and give a correction as in obedience. Always follow with praise to give immediate reassurance that you still love him. For people who are parents, treat them as kindly as you would a child.

Bosco heads back in the house after he has relieved himself. Remember never to allow your puppy inside until after he has eliminated. Owners, the Michals family.

Boxers are so human-like in character, personality and intelligence that they will respond to you because they love to please.

I do urge going to some type of obedience classes. Start with puppy kindergarten classes where there is less demand on the puppy. Check with local trainers. Boxers, being as bright as they are, can easily get bored with repetition and too many demands at a young age. If you own a show puppy and plan to finish his championship title, I don't recommend going through an obedience class. I do, however, recommend show-handling classes which are usually run by a local kennel club or privately by a well-known professional handler. Consult you breeder. It is too big of a demand and the puppy can lose some of its spark, which is an important part of being a "show" dog. I have seen many beautiful show prospects not enjoying the show ring and not attaining their championships.

EAR CROPPING

While many countries, especially those in Europe, have banned ear cropping, it is still legal and routinely done in the United States. Many breeders make it a practice to crop the entire litter between seven to nine weeks of age. This is especially true if the breeder prefers the longer, stylized crop. Ears that are cropped later do not usually stand as well as those that are cropped early. If, for any reason, you want an uncropped Boxer, discuss this with your chosen breeder early as some will not sell uncropped dogs and it is doubtful that you will find older puppies that have not been cropped.

The original reason for cropping the Boxer ears was of a functional nature. While it may no longer serve that purpose in most dogs, it still imparts a specific look to the head.

Thus, from your first Boxer puppy, it is likely that you will need to know how to care for newly cropped ears. The taping and care will continue for a period of several months due to the long, stylized cut that is used in the breed. Over many years of breeding Boxers, I have developed some wonderful methods for

You should provide your Boxer with his own bed. "Aby" proves how quickly a growing Boxer puppy poops out! Owners, Carole and John Hessels.

making them stand properly.

Initially, when the ears are still stitched and healing, apply a medicated powder, which can be found in most drug stores. It should be used twice a day for at least four or five days on the cut edge. This will promote healing and relieve the itchiness that may make a puppy scratch and possibly tear out the stitches.

Once the edge has scabbed over, begin using an aloe vera cream with

Breeders and owners who crop ears must make sure that the puppy's headgear does not interfere with play, an important part of a puppy's development.

Today many owners crop their Boxers' ears, while some choose to leave them natural.

natural vitamin E. After the stitches have been removed, start massaging the ears upward into the position in which you want them to stand. Warm olive oil, an ointment or nothing at all can be used during

the massage. This helps to keep the cut edge stretched during the final healing process as well as making the ear stand more quickly.

Since most Boxer ears do not stand on their own, they will have to be taped. Taping should only be done after the ears have completely healed. Most owners and breeders still use the traditional taping method using a porous cotton tape that will allow the ear to breathe without cutting into the skin.

Most owners and breeders still use the traditional taping method, using a porous cotton tape that will allow the ear to breathe without cutting into the skin.

If the ear flops outward, follow the natural fold of the skin found at the base of the ear. Pull the ear upward, really stretching it, and wrap the tape in a spiral like a barber pole. Taping always begins at the base of the ear. Keep the tape rather loose. If the tape is too tight, it will cut off the circulation to the ear as well as being more difficult to remove. Leave the very tip of the ear exposed as a guide for when you later have to cut the tape off with bandage scissors.

If the ear flops inward, or pulls toward the top of the head, taping will also correct this problem. However, this is a little trickier. First massage the ear with warm olive oil to soften. Then wipe dry with alcohol preps to remove the greasiness and help the tape stick better. Again, start taping from the base of the ear, but, this time, unfold the natural fold of the ear and tape the opposite way from the method described above. This will flip the muscle at the base of the ear so that the ears will straighten upward. Leave the tape on for five to seven days. If left on longer it may cause the muscle to break down. When you remove the tape, let the ear rest for at least a day before retaping. You may want to wait until the ear flops again before repeating the process.

I do not use calcium supplements, but do

recommend vitamin C, which helps to form good connective tissue.

Some owners and breeders have elected to use a relatively new process known as the tapeless method of ear taping. This involves cutting a piece of mole foam to fit inside the ear. The base of the piece is placed solidly inside the base of the ear and secured with skin bond all the way to the top. This keeps the ears stretched and braced. However, you must keep on top of this technique by changing the mole foam every four to five days.

BOXER DIET DIRECTIONS

To keep a Boxer healthy, you must instill good habits, win confidence and obedience through love, feed correctly, and maintain cleanliness of the body and the surroundings.

When you first bring your puppy home, decide what type of food you wish to feed him for the rest of his life. Though Boxers are not subject to intestinal disturbances, sudden changes, especially for puppies, may cause upsets. If your puppy has come a long distance or you take him on a visit, boil the water for about a week, gradually mixing it with local water. When your puppy is accustomed to your water, it is best to bring that water on trips. Let him know that

If you insist on feeding your Boxer human food, wait until he is an adult. Human foods offer poor nutrition for puppies.

the diet you decide upon is his food. Do not leave food for him to eat more than 20 minutes. Do not feed at the table or offer tidbits between meals or cater to whims. Feed puppies and older dogs small amounts frequently rather than one or two large meals. Don't feed table scraps or leftover human food. If you insist on doing so, wait until the Boxer reaches adulthood. Human foods offer poor nutrition for your pup.

When you first bring your puppy home, continue feeding what the breeder recommends. If a change is desired, go about it gradually. Puppy bred by the author.

General directions for diet and sundry suggestions are all subject to your veterinarian's advice. Consult him at once upon observing any unusual symptoms and regularly for general care, annual vaccinations including parvo and coronavirus vaccine and for rabies shot, as well as a monthly heartworm preventative.

The amount to feed is difficult to specify as each individual Boxer varies in basic requirements. Judge by response and conditions. If your dog is ravenous, eats a lot, but does not gain weight, or eats little, has no appetite, and is too thin or fat, consult your veterinarian.

Though some people prefer to feed table scraps, it is better to take advantage of the research reputable feed companies have spent on producing well-balanced complete rations. Of course you can supplement all meals with vitamins, fats, oils and whatever else your dog needs.

The puppy should be given a larger quantity of food than he can eat at each meal. A puppy grows very quickly and adjusts his needs as he grows. If you have left extra food for him, you can easily see when to

increase the quantity. As your puppy matures, you can adjust his meals accordingly.

Brand names sold in pet supply stores are excellent, high quality dry foods and are highly recommended. For puppies lamb and rice dry foods seem to agree with Boxers, resulting in firm stools.

At Jacquet Kennels we recommend this schedule:

Young Puppies: 8 weeks to about 4 months = 4 meals a day

Puppies: 4 months to 6 months = 3 to 4 meals a day

Puppies: 6 months to 1 year = 3 meals a day

Adults: Over 1 year = 2 meals a day.

No matter how perfectly balanced your dog's diet is, he will enjoy sharing a treat with you. Owner, David Rutledge.

CLOSING THOUGHTS

Never tie a Boxer outside. Remember your puppy wants to be where you are and will try very hard to get himself loose. Never allow your dog to run loose, unfenced at any time. Be sure fences and walls cannot be scaled or dug under, and gates must at all times be secure. Guard against a dog running out of house doors.

Keep drugs, poisons, antifreeze and sprays out of your dog's reach. Rat, mice, ant, garden and other poisons and sprays can be fatal, as can articles and walls painted with lead arsenic.

Housebreaking is easy if one is consistent, patient, and persistent. Just as soon as your Boxer can understand,

Always supervise your puppy whenever he is outdoors. Don't let him eat any strange plants or berries, as they may be poisonous.

and he is wiser than you think, teach him good manners and obedience through winning his affection and trust, and through patience, perserverence and praise.

OBEDIENCE Training for Your Boxer

by Karla Spitzer

To get back to Boxers' being smart, how many of you out there really think your Boxer is dumb? If I'm not much mistaken, not many. My dogs can open sliding doors and doors with door knobs. Harpo and Kosmo can pretty much figure out days of the week. They know which days they train and which days they have lessons. (Maybe Cleo can too, but she's not letting on if she can...)

As one of my trainers (Boxer breeder, Liz Farrell) once told me, Boxers were bred for herding, hunting and guarding. In the early days before Frau Stockmann and friends took an interest, they were the indigenous dogs of Europe. They mostly herded, hunted and guarded. They were the "bullbaiters." Remember the story of Frau Stockmann's first dog, Pluto, who took down a stag in his old age? And don't forget all those old pictures from Medieval Europe that had various-sized mastiff-type dogs guarding the castles?

Well, in order to do any of that, you have to have a dog who can scan its horizons. So the dog we know as the modern-day Boxer evolved for centuries to be able to watch his horizons. The Boxer was an independent working dog.

When we take this dog into the obedience ring, its instincts are going to tell it to keep an eye on things for you. Also, I've yet to meet a Boxer who wasn't a quick-take. And most trainers are inclined to want to repeat exercises until it bores most Boxers almost to tears. And a bored Boxer is usually a stubborn Boxer. It's a dog who's saying, "Did that, been there...And I'm not going to do it again. If you want to throw that dumbbell one more time, YOU get it."

Still this isn't all bad. The important thing I've learned in working with my Boxers is that if I can show them very clearly what I want them to do in the first place, it doesn't take that much to teach them. They don't train like the dogs who are generally considered the really "top" obedience competitors, such as Border Collies, Golden Retrievers, German Shepherds, Poodles and Shelties. Except for Poodles, the rest are all sporting or herding dogs. These are dogs who were bred to work very closely with man.

Boxers, I feel, have a much wider range of interest. And often, I find that they will learn a great deal by watching (so make sure they're watching good dogs!). This is not always good news when it comes to training for obedience. But it is good to know about how your "off-breed obedience dog" learns.

It is believed that Boxers have a stubborn personality. In order to get your Boxer's head out of the sand, you have to make training fun and exciting.

Your Boxer will probably

never retrieve a stick out of water as often as a Golden Retriever, or chase a ball as often as a Border Collie. However, if you'll respect the intelligence and nobility that your dog has, you can have a fine competitive obedience dog nevertheless. You've got a dog who is smarter in more areas than most, you just need to be more creative in getting him or her to work with you. Once I learned that if Harpo did something well one time and let it go at that instead of repeating things, we really began accelerating in our ability and our trial scores.

What happens with most Boxers if you repeat things too much in one session is that they'll decide one of two things. (1) Since they've already done it, even if they've done it right, something must be wrong, so they'll do it differently. (2) Since they've already done it, it's

The choke collar is commonly used in training. Always use it with care. This is Susancar Barry owned by Sandra Carter, England.

One theory on the origin of the breed's name claims that it can be traced back to the dog's way of extending his front paws like a professional Boxer when playing.

boring, and they'll try to make it more interesting, therefore do it differently.

So since what you wanted was more of the same, getting multiple repeats can be pretty self-defeating. My advice? Don't do it. If you like to do the same things over and over again, get a Border Collie or a Golden Retriever. If you want an efficient dog, get a Boxer

A little tip on going into classes with your Boxer: If you live in an area where there aren't any other Boxers showing, you can assume that no one in the area really knows how to train them. There are always Boxers around, but a lot of trainers don't have a lot of experience with them or other members of the Working Group. If the trainer you're considering taking lessons with says things like, "Boxers are stubborn, they'll never do it," etc., consider going elsewhere. If they have a sense of humor and seem good with dogs in general, you might want to stay. If they say you can only train a Boxer with a "pinch collar and a cattle prod," run the other way. You can bet your Boxer will!

Unless your dog is totally vicious, people-aggressive, ill-bred, or so dominant that you're frightened of it, don't let anyone tell you your dog is bad, stubborn or stupid. If it's not doing what you want, you just haven't built up the communication skills to let it know what to do to please you. Even though the general belief is that Boxers are stubborn, I think that it's more that they're watchful, careful and economical with their movements and decisions. And frankly, I think that's a good attribute of the breed. If you go on with obedience, you will find there are many areas where there are differences from the popular obedience breeds.

For instance, if you attempt to teach your Boxer moving and stationary attention, remember that you will probably not get the same "appearance" of attention as the so-called "hot" obedience breeds. Some of those Border Collies, Goldens and Aussies can wrap their heads right around in front of their handlers and look like they're glued to their handler's thighs! Boxers don't have that level of neck flexibility or interest, besides in their own

Who needs a cue? Boxers are very intelligent. This is Jacquet's Little Miss Magic owned by Jeff and Missy Mathis and Rick Tomita.

little heart of hearts they *know* their real job is to watch out for you. Nevertheless, when they understand the concept of attention and that it is their job to watch you while staying in the heel position, they can give you the same precision that any other breed can. They just won't be as obvious about looking at you. And I feel it is their nature, if they aren't lacking in self-confidence, to heel a little wider.

Teaching your Boxer to swim is an easy task and essential if you have a swimming pool in your yard. Always supervise a dog in a pool—and teach him how to get out!

Since a Boxer can jump, do agility, and think on his toes, there is no reason why you can't go as far as you like in any of the dog sports. You just need to respect your particular dog's abilities, and not lump him or her into too many "dog" categories (too stubborn, too slow, too stupid, and so on). You might find out that he/she is just a little too smart and has you all figured out. And far be it from any Boxer to disappoint its owner if the owner thinks the Boxer can't do something. This is one of the almost scary aspects of Boxers. If you think your dog can't do something, it won't. If you think it can, it will. I've seen this time and time again when I'm working with friends to try to train their dogs. The dog will almost always do what I want with no force or fight, and just a bit of encouragement, thus totally amazing their owners. It's because I *believe* they can do it. I think Boxers are *very* intuitive. This is one area where if you think your dog can do it, it can and will do it but not without some reasonable and thoughtful training, of course...

SPORT of Purebred Dogs

Welcome to the exciting and sometimes frustrating sport of dogs. No doubt you are trying to learn more about dogs or you wouldn't be deep into this book. This section covers the basics that may entice you, further your knowledge and help you to understand the dog world. If you decide to give showing, obedience or any other dog activities a try, then I suggest you seek further help from the appropriate source.

Dog showing has been a very popular sport for a long time and has been taken quite seriously by some. Others only enjoy it as a hobby.

The Kennel Club in England was formed in 1859, the American Kennel Club was established in 1884 and the Canadian Kennel Club was formed in 1888. The purpose of these clubs was to register purebred dogs and maintain their Stud Books. In the beginning, the concept of registering dogs was not readily accepted. More than 36 million dogs have been enrolled in the AKC Stud Book since its inception in 1888. Presently the kennel clubs not only register dogs but adopt and enforce rules and regulations governing dog shows, obedience trials and field trials. Over the years they have fostered and encouraged interest in the health and welfare of the purebred dog. They routinely donate funds to veterinary research for study on genetic disorders.

Below are the addresses of the kennel clubs in the United States, Great Britain and Canada.

The American Kennel Club
51 Madison Avenue
New York, NY 10010
(Their registry is located at: 5580 Centerview Drive, STE 200, Raleigh, NC 27606-3390)

The Kennel Club
1 Clarges Street
Piccadilly, London, WIY 8AB, England

The Canadian Kennel Club
111 Eglinton Avenue
East Toronto, Ontario M6S 4V7
Canada

Today there are numerous activities that are enjoyable for both the dog and the handler. Some of the activities include conformation showing, obedience competition, agility, tracking, the Canine Good Citizen Certificate, and a wide range of instinct tests that vary from breed to breed. Where you start depends upon your goals which early on may not be readily apparent.

This is Kay Palade in the ring with Ch. Vancroft's Prime Time owned by Deborah Clark and Marcia Adams.

CONFORMATION

Conformation showing is our oldest dog show sport. This type of showing is based on the dog's appearance—that is his structure, movement and attitude. When considering this type of

showing, you need to be aware of your breed's standard and be able to evaluate your dog compared to that standard. The breeder of your puppy or other experienced breeders would be good sources for such an evaluation. Puppies can go through lots of changes over a period of time. I always say most puppies start out as promising hopefuls and then after maturing may be disappointing as show candidates. Even so this should not deter them from being excellent pets.

Usually conformation training classes are offered by the local kennel or obedience clubs. These are excellent places for training puppies. The puppy should be able to walk on a lead before entering such a class. Proper ring procedure and technique for posing (stacking) the dog will be demonstrated as well as gaiting the dog. Usually certain patterns are used in the ring such as the triangle or the "L." Conformation class, like the PKT class, will give your youngster the opportunity to socialize with different breeds of dogs and humans too.

It takes some time to learn the routine of conformation showing. Usually one starts at the puppy matches which may be AKC Sanctioned or Fun Matches. These matches are generally for puppies from two or three months to a year old, and there may be classes for the adult over the age of 12 months. Similar to point shows, the classes are divided by sex and after completion of the classes in that breed or variety, the class winners compete for Best of Breed or Variety. The winner goes on to compete in the Group and the Group winners compete for Best in Match. No championship points are awarded for match wins.

Earning a championship in England is different than in the U.S. or Canada, as there is no point system. A Challenge Certificate is awarded if the judge feels the dog is deserving.

A few matches can be great training for puppies even though there is no intention to go on showing. Matches enable the puppy to meet new people and be handled by a stranger—the judge. It is also a change of environment, which broadens the horizon for both dog and handler. Matches and other dog activities boost the confidence of the handler and especially the younger handlers.

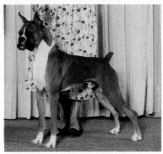

Ch. Jacquet's Millennium winning Best Puppy in Working Group at eight months of age.

Earning an AKC championship is built on a point system, which is different from Great Britain. To become an AKC Champion of Record the dog must earn 15 points. The number of points earned each time depends upon the number of dogs in competition. The number of points available at each show depends upon the breed, its sex and the location of the show. The United States is divided into ten AKC zones. Each zone has its own set of points. The purpose of the zones is to try to equalize the points available from breed to breed and area to area. The AKC adjusts the point scale annually.

The number of points that can be won at a show are between one and five. Three-, four- and five-point wins are considered majors. Not only does the dog need 15 points won under three different judges, but those points must include two majors under two different judges. Canada also works on a point system but majors are not required.

Junior Showmanship

The Junior Showmanship Class is a wonderful way to build self confidence even if there are no aspirations of staying with the dog-show game later in life. Frequently, Junior Showmanship becomes the background of those who become successful exhibitors/handlers in the future. In some instances it is taken very seriously, and success is measured in terms of wins. The Junior Handler is judged solely on his ability and skill in presenting his dog. The dog's conformation is not to be considered by the judge.

Even so the condition and grooming of the dog may be a reflection upon the handler.

CANINE GOOD CITIZEN

The AKC sponsors a program to encourage dog owners to train their dogs. Local clubs perform the pass/fail tests, and dogs who pass are awarded a Canine Good Citizen Certificate. Proof of vaccination is required at the time of participation. The test includes:

1. Accepting a friendly stranger.
2. Sitting politely for petting.
3. Appearance and grooming.
4. Walking on a loose leash.
5. Walking through a crowd.
6. Sit and down on command/ staying in place.
7. Come when called.
8. Reaction to another dog.
9. Reactions to distractions.
10. Supervised separation.

Rebecca Bradshaw is a successful junior handler. She is shown here with Aust. Ch. Ozstock Rags To Riches owned and bred by Dianne and Dennis Bradshaw.

If more effort was made by pet owners to accomplish these exercises, fewer dogs would be cast off to the humane shelter.

OBEDIENCE

Obedience is necessary, without a doubt, but it can also become a wonderful hobby or even an obsession. In my opinion, obedience classes and competition can provide wonderful companionship, not only with your dog but with your classmates or fellow competitors. It is always gratifying to discuss your dog's problems with others who have had similar experiences. The AKC acknowledged Obedience around 1936, and it has changed tremendously even though many of the exercises are basically the same. Today, obedience competition is just that—very competitive. Even so, it is possible for every obedience exhibitor to come home a winner (by earning qualifying scores) even though he/she may not earn a placement in the class.

TRACKING

Tracking is officially classified obedience, but I feel it

should have its own category. There are three tracking titles available: Tracking Dog (TD), Tracking Dog Excellent (TDX), Variable Surface Tracking (VST). If all three tracking titles are obtained, then the dog officially becomes a CT (Champion Tracker). The CT will go in front of the dog's name.

A TD may be earned anytime and does not have to follow the other obedience titles. There are many exhibitors that prefer tracking to obedience, and there are others like myself that do both. In my experience with small dogs, I prefer to earn the CD and CDX before attempting tracking. My reasoning is that small dogs

Boxer leaping through the tire jump in an agility trial. Owner, Ella M. DuPree.

are closer to the mat in the obedience rings and therefore it's too easy to put the nose down and sniff. Tracking encourages sniffing. Of course this depends on the dog. I've had some dogs that tracked around the ring and others (TDXs) who wouldn't think of sniffing in the ring.

AGILITY

Agility was first introduced by John Varley in England at the Crufts Dog Show, February 1978, but Peter Meanwell, competitor and judge, actually developed the idea. It was officially recognized in the early '80s. Agility is extremely popular in England and Canada and growing in popularity in the U.S. The AKC acknowledged agility in August 1994. Dogs must be at least 12 months of age to be entered. It is a fascinating sport that the dog, handler and spectators enjoy to the utmost. Agility is a spectator sport! The dog performs

A Boxer sails over the bar jump at an agility trial. Agility is a sport that is fun for dogs, owners, and spectators alike. Owner, Ella M. DuPree.

off lead. The handler either runs with his dog or positions himself on the course and directs his dog with verbal and hand signals over a timed course over or through a variety of obstacles including a time out or pause. One of the main drawbacks to agility is finding a place to train. The obstacles take up a lot of space and it is very time consuming to put up and take down courses.

The titles earned at AKC agility trials are Novice Agility Dog (NAD), Open Agility Dog (OAD), Agility Dog Excellent (ADX), and Master Agility Excellent (MAX). In order to acquire an agility title, a dog must earn a qualifying score in its respective class on three separate occasions under two different judges. The MAX will be awarded after earning ten qualifying scores in the Agility Excellent Class.

Schutzhund

The German word "Schutzhund" translated to English means "Protection Dog." It is a fast growing competitive sport in the United States and has been popular in England since the early 1900s. Schutzhund was originally a test to determine which German Shepherds were quality dogs for breeding in Germany. It gives us the ability to test our dogs for correct temperament and working ability. Like every other dog sport, it requires teamwork between the handler and the dog.

Schutzhund training and showing involves three phases: Tracking, Obedience and Protection. There are three SchH levels: SchH I (novice), SchH II (intermediate), and SchH III (advanced). Each title becomes progressively more difficult. The handler and dog start out in each phase with 100 points. Points are deducted as errors are incurred. A total perfect score is 300, and for a dog and handler to earn a title he must earn at least 70 points in tracking and obedience and at least 80 points in protection. Today many different breeds participate successfully in Schutzhund.

General Information

Obedience, tracking and agility allow the purebred dog with an Indefinite Listing Privilege (ILP) number or a limited registration to be exhibited and earn titles. Application must be made to the AKC for an ILP number.

The American Kennel Club publishes a monthly *events* magazine that is part of the *Gazette*, their official journal for the sport of purebred dogs. The *Events* section lists upcoming shows and the secretary or superintendent for them. The majority of the conformation shows in the U.S. are overseen by licensed superintendents. Generally the entry closing date is approximately two-and-a-half weeks before the actual show. Point shows are fairly expensive, while the match shows cost about one third of the point show entry fee.

Although many Boxers in Europe are trained in Schutzhund, the practice is generally frowned upon by American and British fanciers.

Match shows usually take entries the day of the show but some are pre-entry. The best way to find match show information is through your local kennel club. Upon asking, the AKC can provide you with a list of superintendents, and you can write and ask to be put on their mailing lists.

Obedience trial and tracking test information is available through the AKC. Frequently these events are not superintended, but put on by the host club. Therefore you would make the entry with the event's secretary.

As you have read, there are numerous activities you can share with your dog. Regardless what you do, it does take teamwork. Your dog can only benefit from your attention and training. I hope this chapter has enlightened you and hope, if nothing else, you will attend a show here and there. Perhaps you will start with a puppy kindergarten class, and who knows where it may lead!

HEALTH CARE for Your Boxer

Veterinary medicine has become far more sophisticated than what was available to our ancestors. This can be attributed to the increase in household pets and consequently the demand for better care for them. Also human medicine has become far more complex. Today diagnostic testing in veterinary medicine parallels human diagnostics. Because of better technology we can expect our pets to live healthier lives thereby increasing their life spans.

Laboratory tests are studied by highly trained veterinary technicians. Most tests are performed right in your own veterinarian's office.

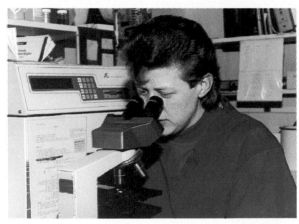

THE FIRST CHECK UP

You will want to take your new puppy/dog in for its first check up within 48 to 72 hours after acquiring it. Many breeders strongly recommend this check up and so do the humane shelters. A puppy/dog can appear healthy but it may have a serious problem that is not apparent to the layman. Most pets have some type of a minor flaw that may never cause a real problem.

Unfortunately if he/she should have a serious problem, you will want to consider the consequences of keeping the pet and the attachments that will be formed, which may be broken prematurely. Keep in mind there are many healthy dogs looking for good homes.

Chief the Boxer being caressed by a foster-cared raccoon orphan. Wild raccoons carry the rabies virus and should not come in contact with your dog. Owner, Cynthia S. White.

This first check up is a good time to establish yourself with the veterinarian and learn the office policy regarding their hours and how they handle emergencies. Usually the breeder or another conscientious pet owner is a good reference for locating a capable veterinarian. You should be aware that not all veterinarians give the same quality of service. Please do not make your selection on the least expensive clinic, as they may be short changing your pet. There is the possibility that eventually it will cost you more due to improper diagnosis, treatment, etc. If you are selecting a new veterinarian, feel free to ask for a tour of the clinic. You should inquire about making an appointment for a tour since all clinics are working clinics, and therefore may not be available all day for sightseers.

You may worry less if you see where your pet will be spending the day if he ever needs to be hospitalized.

THE PHYSICAL EXAM

Your veterinarian will check your pet's overall condition, which includes listening to the heart; checking the respiration; feeling the abdomen, muscles and joints; checking the mouth, which includes the gum color and signs of gum disease along with plaque buildup; checking the ears for signs of an infection or ear mites; examining the eyes; and, last but not least, checking the condition of the skin and coat.

A good veterinarian can always be counted on. This veterinarian is administering to a sore paw resulting from stepping on a lighted cigarette.

He should ask you questions regarding your pet's eating and elimination habits and invite you to relay your questions. It is a good idea to prepare a list so as not to forget anything. He should discuss the proper diet and the quantity to be fed. If this should differ from your breeder's recommendation, then you should convey to him the breeder's choice and see if he approves. If he recommends changing the diet, then this should be done over a few days so as not to cause a gastrointestinal upset. It is customary to take in a fresh stool sample (just

Boxer puppies receive maternal antibodies via their mother's milk until the ages of 12 to 18 weeks.

106

a small amount) for a test for intestinal parasites. It must be fresh, preferably within 12 hours, since the eggs hatch quickly and after hatching will not be observed under the microscope. If your pet isn't obliging then, usually the technician can take one in the clinic.

IMMUNIZATIONS

It is important that you take your puppy/dog's vaccination record with you on your first visit. In case of a puppy, presumably the breeder has seen to the vaccinations up to the time you acquired custody. Veterinarians differ in their vaccination protocol. It is not unusual for your puppy to have received vaccinations for distemper, hepatitis, leptospirosis, parvovirus and parainfluenza every two to three weeks from the age of five or six weeks. Usually this is a combined injection and is typically called the DHLPP. The DHLPP is given through at least 12 to 14 weeks of age, and it is customary to continue with another parvovirus vaccine at 16 to 18 weeks. You may wonder why so many immunizations are necessary. No one knows for sure when the puppy's maternal antibodies are gone, although it is customarily accepted that distemper antibodies are gone by 12 weeks. Usually parvovirus antibodies are gone by 16 to 18 weeks of age. However, it is possible for the maternal antibodies to be gone at a much earlier age or even a later age. Therefore immunizations are started at an early age. The vaccine will not give immunity as long as there are maternal antibodies.

The rabies vaccination is given at three or six months of age depending on your local laws. A vaccine for bordetella (kennel cough) is advisable and can be given anytime from the age of five weeks. The coronavirus is not commonly given unless there is a problem locally. The Lyme vaccine is necessary in endemic areas. Lyme disease has been reported in 47 states.

Distemper

This is virtually an incurable disease. If the dog recovers, he is subject to severe nervous disorders. The virus attacks every tissue in the body and resembles a bad cold with a fever. It can cause a runny nose and eyes and cause gastrointestinal disorders, including a poor appetite, vomiting and diarrhea. The virus is carried by raccoons, foxes, wolves, mink and other dogs. Unvaccinated youngsters and senior citizens are very susceptible. This is still a common disease.

Hepatitis

This is a virus that is most serious in very young dogs. It is spread by contact with an infected animal or its stool or urine. The virus affects the liver and kidneys and is characterized by high fever, depression and lack of appetite. Recovered animals may be afflicted with chronic illnesses.

This pup was a "fading" puppy. It is getting a boost of sterile electrolyte fluid under the skin to hydrate it.

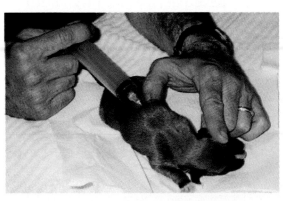

Leptospirosis

This is a bacterial disease transmitted by contact with the urine of an infected dog, rat or other wildlife. It produces severe symptoms of fever, depression, jaundice and internal bleeding and was fatal before the vaccine was developed. Recovered dogs can be carriers, and the disease can be transmitted from dogs to humans.

Parvovirus

This was first noted in the late 1970s and is still a fatal disease. However, with proper vaccinations, early diagnosis and prompt treatment, it is a manageable disease. It attacks the bone marrow and intestinal tract. The symptoms include depression, loss of appetite, vomiting, diarrhea and collapse. Immediate medical attention is of the essence.

Rabies

This is shed in the saliva and is carried by raccoons, skunks, foxes, other dogs and cats. It attacks nerve tissue, resulting in paralysis and death. Rabies can be transmitted to people and is virtually always fatal. This disease is reappearing in the suburbs.

Bordetella (Kennel Cough)

The symptoms are coughing, sneezing, hacking and retching accompanied by nasal discharge usually lasting from a few days to several weeks. There are several disease-producing organisms responsible for this disease. The present vaccines are helpful but do not protect for all the strains. It usually is not life threatening but in some instances it can progress to a serious bronchopneumonia. The disease is highly contagious. The vaccination should be given routinely for dogs that come in contact with other dogs, such as through boarding, training class or visits to the groomer.

Coronavirus

This is usually self limiting and not life threatening. It was first noted in the late '70s about a year before parvovirus. The virus produces a yellow/brown stool and there may be depression, vomiting and diarrhea.

Lyme Disease

This was first diagnosed in the United States in 1976 in

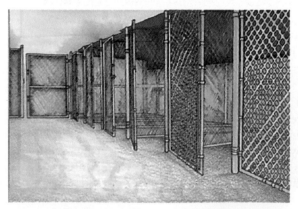

A reputable boarding kennel will require that dogs receive the vaccination for kennel cough no less than two weeks before their scheduled stay.

Lyme, CT in people who lived in close proximity to the deer tick. Symptoms may include acute lameness, fever, swelling of joints and loss of appetite. Your veterinarian can advise you if you live in an endemic area.

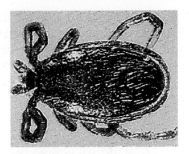

The deer tick is the most common carrier of Lyme disease. Photo courtesy of Virbac Laboratories, Inc., Fort Worth, Texas.

After your puppy has completed his puppy vaccinations, you will continue to booster the DHLPP once a year. It is customary to booster the rabies one year after the first vaccine and then, depending on where you live, it should be boostered every year or every three years. This depends on your local laws. The Lyme and corona vaccines are boostered annually and it is recommended that the bordetella be boostered every six to eight months.

ANNUAL VISIT

I would like to impress the importance of the annual check up, which would include the booster vaccinations, check for intestinal parasites and test for heartworm. Today in our very busy world it is rush, rush and see "how much you can get for how little." Unbelievably, some non-veterinary businesses have entered into the vaccination business. More harm than good can come to your dog through improper vaccinations, possibly from inferior vaccines and/or the wrong schedule. More than likely you truly care about your companion dog and over the years you have devoted much time and expense to his well being. Perhaps you are unaware that a vaccination is not just a vaccination. There is more involved. Please, please follow through with regular physical examinations. It is so important for your veterinarian to know your dog and this is especially true during middle age through the geriatric years. More than likely your older dog will require more than one physical a year. The annual physical is good preventive medicine. Through early diagnosis and subsequent treatment your dog can maintain a longer and better quality of life.

INTESTINAL PARASITES

Hookworms

These are an almost microscopic intestinal worms that can cause anemia and therefore serious problems, including death, in young puppies. Hookworms can be transmitted to humans through penetration of the skin. Puppies may be born with them.

Roundworms

These are spaghetti-like worms that can cause a potbellied appearance and dull coat along with more severe symptoms, such as vomiting, diarrhea and coughing. Puppies acquire these while in the mother's uterus and through lactation. Both hookworms and roundworms may be acquired through ingestion.

Whipworms

These have a three-month life cycle and are not acquired through the dam. They cause intermittent diarrhea usually with mucus. Whipworms are possibly the most difficult worm to eradicate. Their eggs are very resistant to most environmental factors and can last for years until the proper conditions enable them to mature. Whipworms are seldom seen in the stool.

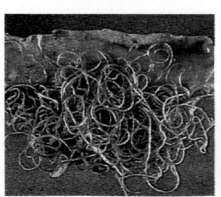

Roundworms are spaghetti-like worms that cause a potbellied appearance and dull coat. More severe symptoms can be diarrhea and vomiting. Photo courtesy of Merck AgVet.

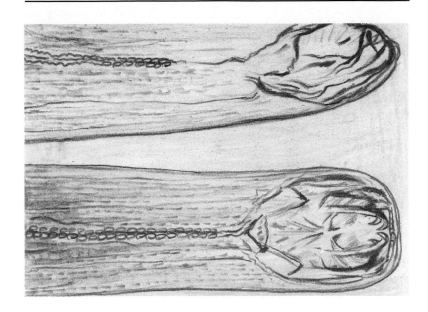

Hookworms are almost microscopic intestinal worms that can cause anemia and therefore serious problems, including death.

Intestinal parasites are more prevalent in some areas than others. Climate, soil and contamination are big factors contributing to the incidence of intestinal parasites. Eggs are passed in the stool, lay on the ground and then become infective in a certain number of days. Each of the above worms has a different life cycle. Your best chance of becoming and remaining worm-free is to always pooper-scoop your yard. A fenced-in yard keeps stray dogs out, which is certainly helpful.

I would recommend having a fecal examination on your dog twice a year or more often if there is a problem. If your dog has a positive fecal sample, then he will be given the appropriate medication and you will be asked to bring back another stool sample in a certain period of time (depending on the type of worm) and then be rewormed. This process goes on until he has at least two negative samples. The different types of worms require different medications. You will be wasting your money and doing your dog an injustice by buying over-the-counter medication without first consulting your veterinarian.

OTHER INTERNAL PARASITES

Coccidiosis and Giardiasis

These protozoal infections usually affect puppies, especially in places where large numbers of puppies are brought together. Older dogs may harbor these infections but do not show signs unless they are stressed. Symptoms include diarrhea, weight loss and lack of appetite. These infections are not always apparent in the fecal examination.

Tapeworms

Seldom apparent on fecal floatation, they are diagnosed frequently as rice-like segments around the dog's anus and the base of the tail. Tapeworms are long, flat and ribbon like, sometimes several feet in length, and made up of many segments about five-eighths of an inch long. The two most common types of tapeworms found in the dog are:

(1) First the larval form of the flea tapeworm parasite must mature in an intermediate host, the flea, before it can become infective. Your dog acquires this by ingesting the flea through licking and chewing.

(2) Rabbits, rodents and certain large game animals serve as intermediate hosts for other species of tapeworms. If your dog should eat one of these infected hosts, then he can acquire tapeworms.

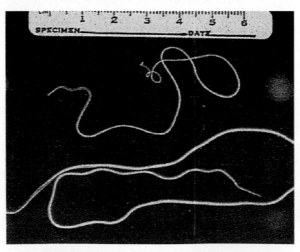

Adult male and female heartworms. Heartworm is a life-threatening disease that is expensive to treat and easily prevented. Photo courtesy of Merck AgVet.

Heartworm Disease

This is a worm that resides in the heart and adjacent blood vessels of the lung that produces microfilaria, which circulate in the bloodstream. It is possible for a dog to be infected with any number of worms from one to a hundred that can be 6 to 14 inches long. It is a life-threatening disease, expensive to treat and easily prevented. Depending on where you live, your veterinarian may recommend a preventive year-round and either an annual or semiannual blood test. The most common preventive is given once a month.

The cat flea is the most common flea of both dogs and cats. Courtesy of Fleabusters, Rx for Fleas, Inc., Fort Lauderdale, Florida.

Diagram of the cat flea. Courtesy of Fleabusters, Rx for Fleas, Inc., Fort Lauderdale, Florida.

External Parasites

Fleas

These pests are not only the dog's worst

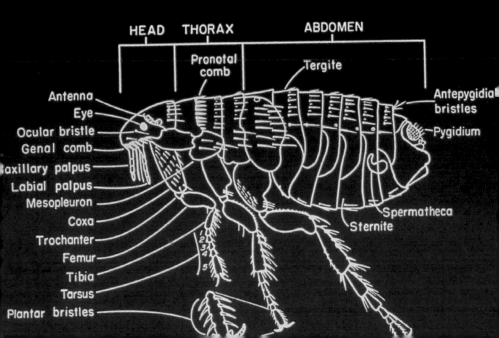

DIAGRAM OF FLEA

enemy but also enemy to the owner's pocketbook. Preventing is less expensive than treating, but regardless I think we'd prefer to spend our money elsewhere. I would guess that the majority of our dogs are allergic to the bite of a flea, and in many cases it only takes one flea bite. The protein in the flea's saliva is the culprit. Allergic dogs have a reaction, which usually results in a "hot spot." More than likely such a reaction will involve a trip to the veterinarian for treatment. Yes, prevention is less expensive. Fortunately today there are several good products available.

If there is a flea infestation, no one product is going to correct the problem. Not only will the dog require treatment so will the environment. In general flea collars are not very effective although there is now available an "egg" collar that will kill the eggs on the dog. Dips are the most economical

Under ideal conditions fleas can complete their life cycle in three weeks. Courtesy of Fleabusters, Rx for Fleas, Inc., Fort Lauderdale, Florida.

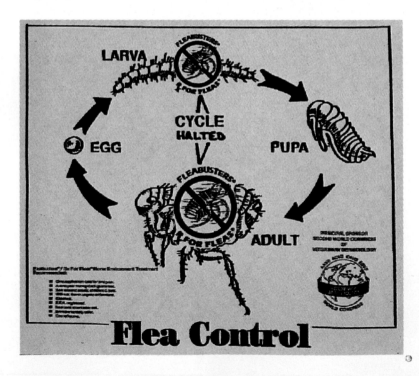

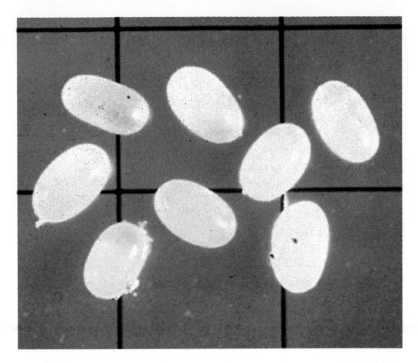

Flea eggs are laid on the dog but easily fall off into the environment and must be eradicated. Courtesy of Fleabusters, Rx for Fleas, Inc., Fort Lauderdale, Florida.

but they are messy. There are some effective shampoos and treatments available through pet shops and veterinarians. An oral tablet arrived on the American market in 1995 and was popular in Europe the previous year. It sterilizes the female flea but will not kill adult fleas. Therefore the tablet, which is given monthly, will decrease the flea population but is not a "cure-all." Those dogs that suffer from flea-bite allergy will still be subjected to the bite of the flea. Another popular parasiticide is permethrin, which is applied to the back of the dog in one or two places depending on the dog's weight. This product works as a repellent causing the flea to get "hot feet" and jump off. Do not confuse this product with some of the organophosphates that are also applied to the dog's back.

Some products are not usable on young puppies. Treating fleas should be done under your veterinarian's guidance. Frequently it is necessary to combine products and the layman does not have the knowledge regarding possible toxicities. It is hard to believe but there are a few dogs that do have a natural resistance to fleas. Nevertheless it would be wise to treat all pets at the same time. Don't forget your cats. Cats just love to prowl the neighborhood and consequently return with unwanted guests.

Adult fleas live on the dog but their eggs drop off the dog into the environment. There they go through four larval stages before reaching adulthood, and thereby are able to jump back on the poor unsuspecting dog. The cycle resumes and takes between 21 to 28 days under ideal conditions. There are environmental products available that will kill both the adult fleas and the larvae.

Ticks

Ticks carry Rocky Mountain Spotted Fever, Lyme disease and can cause tick paralysis. They should be removed with tweezers, trying to pull out the head. The jaws carry disease. There is a tick preventive collar that does an excellent job. The ticks automatically back out on those dogs wearing collars.

Sarcoptic Mange

This is a mite that is difficult to find on skin scrapings. The pinnal reflex is a good indicator of this disease. Rub the ends of the pinna (ear) together and the dog will start scratching with his foot. Sarcoptes are highly contagious to

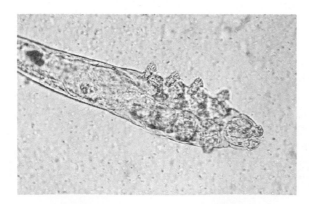

The demodex mite is passed from the dam to her puppies. It affects youngsters from the ages of three to ten months.

other dogs and to humans although they do not live long on humans. They cause intense itching.

Demodectic Mange

This is a mite that is passed from the dam to her puppies. It affects youngsters age three to ten months. Diagnosis is confirmed by skin scraping. Small areas of alopecia around the eyes, lips and/or forelegs become visible. There is little itching unless there is a secondary bacterial infection. Some breeds are afflicted more than others.

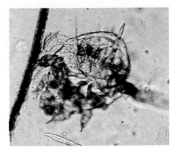

Sarcoptes are highly contagious to other dogs and to humans, although they do not live long on humans. They cause intense itching.

Cheyletiella

This causes intense itching and is diagnosed by skin scraping. It lives in the outer layers of the skin of dogs, cats, rabbits and humans. Yellow-gray scales may be found on the back and the rump, top of the head and the nose.

TO BREED OR NOT TO BREED

More than likely your breeder has requested that you have your puppy neutered or spayed. Your breeder's request is based on what is healthiest for your dog and what is most beneficial for your breed. Experienced and conscientious breeders devote many years into developing a bloodline. In order to do this, he makes every effort to plan each breeding in regard to conformation, temperament and health. This type of breeder does his best to perform the necessary testing (i.e., OFA, CERF, testing for inherited blood disorders, thyroid, etc.). Testing is expensive and sometimes very disheartening when a favorite dog doesn't pass his health tests. The health history pertains not only to the breeding stock but to the immediate ancestors. Reputable breeders do not want their offspring to be bred indiscriminately. Therefore you may be asked to neuter or spay your puppy. Of course there is always the exception, and your breeder may agree to let you breed your dog under his direct supervision. This is an important concept. More and more effort is being made to breed healthier dogs.

Spay/Neuter

There are numerous benefits of performing this surgery at six months of age. An unspayed female is subject to mammary and ovarian cancer. In order to prevent mammary cancer she must be spayed prior to her first heat cycle. Later in life, an unspayed female may develop a pyometra (an infected uterus), which is definitely life threatening.

Spaying is performed under a general anesthetic and is easy on the young dog. As you might expect it is a little harder on the older dog, but that is no reason to deny her the surgery. The surgery removes the ovaries and uterus. It is important to remove all the ovarian tissue. If some is left behind, she could remain attractive to males. In order to view the ovaries, a reasonably long incision is necessary. An ovariohysterectomy is considered major surgery.

Neutering the male at a young age will inhibit some characteristic male behavior that owners frown upon. I have found my boys will not hike their legs and mark territory if they are neutered at six months of age. Also neutering at a young age has hormonal benefits, lessening the chance of hormonal aggressiveness.

Surgery involves removing the testicles but leaving the scrotum. If there should be a retained testicle, then he definitely needs to be neutered before the age of two or three years. Retained testicles can develop into cancer. Unneutered males are at risk for testicular cancer, perineal fistulas, perianal tumors and fistulas and prostatic disease.

Intact males and females are prone to housebreaking accidents. Females urinate frequently before, during and after heat cycles, and males tend to mark territory if there is a female in heat. Males may show the same behavior if there is a visiting dog or guests.

Surgery involves a sterile operating procedure equivalent to human surgery. The incision site is shaved, surgically scrubbed and draped. The veterinarian wears a sterile surgical gown, cap, mask and gloves. Anesthesia should be monitored by a registered technician. It is customary for the veterinarian to recommend a pre-anesthetic blood screening, looking for metabolic problems and a ECG rhythm strip to check for normal heart function. Today anesthetics are equal to human anesthetics, which enables your dog to walk out of the clinic the same day as surgery.

Some folks worry about their dog's gaining weight after being neutered or spayed. This is usually not the case. It is true that some dogs may be less active so they could develop a problem, but my own dogs are just as active as they were before surgery. I have a hard time keeping weight on them. However, if your dog should begin to gain, then you need to decrease his food and see to it that he gets a little more exercise.

If you are not fully prepared for the extensive cost and care of breeding your Boxer bitch, you should have her spayed.

DENTAL CARE for Your Dog's Life

So you've got a new puppy! You also have a new set of puppy teeth in your household. Anyone who has ever raised a puppy is abundantly aware of these new teeth. Your puppy will chew anything it can reach, chase your shoelaces, and play "tear the rag" with any piece of clothing it can find. When puppies are newly born, they have no teeth. At about four weeks of age, puppies of most breeds begin to develop their deciduous or baby teeth. They begin eating semi-solid food, fighting and biting with their litter mates, and learning discipline from their mother. As their new teeth come in, they inflict more pain on their mother's breasts, so her feeding sessions become less frequent and shorter. By six or eight weeks, the mother will start growling to warn her pups when they are fighting too roughly or hurting her as they nurse too much with their new teeth.

Nylabones® not only give your Boxer a good chewing workout but also help to save his teeth. Owner, Rick Tomita.

Puppies need to chew. It is a necessary part of their physical and mental development. They develop muscles and necessary life skills as they drag objects around, fight over possession, and vocalize alerts and warnings. Puppies chew on things to explore their world. They are using their sense of taste to determine what is food and what is not. How else can they tell an electrical cord from a lizard? At about four months of age, most puppies begin shedding their baby teeth.

Playing with a Nylaball® is great fun for your Boxer puppy. Balls made of nylon are practically indestructible. This is Jeff Michals and Bosco.

Often these teeth need some help to come out and make way for the permanent teeth. The incisors (front teeth) will be replaced first. Then, the adult canine or fang teeth erupt. When the baby tooth is not shed before the permanent tooth comes in, veterinarians call it a retained deciduous tooth. This condition will often cause gum infections by trapping hair and debris between the permanent tooth and the retained baby tooth. Nylafloss® is an excellent device for puppies to use. They can toss it, drag it, and chew on the many surfaces it presents. The baby teeth can catch in the nylon material, aiding in their removal. Puppies that have adequate chew toys will have less destructive behavior, develop more physically, and have less chance of retained deciduous teeth.

During the first year, your dog should be seen by your veterinarian at regular intervals. Your veterinarian will let you know when to bring in your puppy for vaccinations and parasite examinations. At each visit, your veterinarian should inspect the lips, teeth, and mouth as part of a complete physical examination. You should take some part in the maintenance of your dog's oral health. You should examine your dog's mouth weekly throughout his first year to make sure there are no sores, foreign objects, tooth problems, etc. If your dog drools excessively, shakes its head, or has bad breath, consult your veterinarian. By the time your dog is six months old, the permanent teeth are all in and plaque can start to accumulate on the tooth surfaces. This is when your dog needs to develop good dental-care habits

These puppies, bred by the author, are sharing a Gumabone® Wishbone. These chew toys come in a variety of shapes and colors and Boxers love to chew them.

to prevent calculus build-up on its teeth. Brushing is best. That is a fact that cannot be denied. However, some dogs do not like their teeth brushed regularly, or you may not be able to accomplish the task. In that case, you should consider a product that will help prevent plaque and calculus build-up.

Never give your Boxer a cotton tug toy, as cotton is organic and rots.

The Plaque Attackers® and Galileo Bone® are other excellent choices for the first three years of a dog's life. Their shapes make them interesting for the dog. As the dog chews on them, the solid polyurethane

Nylafloss® is an excellent device for puppies to use. They can toss it, drag it, and chew on it.

massages the gums which improves the blood circulation to the periodontal tissues. Projections on the chew devices increase the surface and are in contact with the tooth for more efficient cleaning.

The unique shape and consistency prevent your dog from exerting excessive force on his own teeth or from breaking off pieces of the bone. If your dog is an aggressive chewer or weighs more than 55 pounds (25 kg), you should consider giving him a Nylabone®, the most durable chew product on the market.

The Gumabone®, made by the Nylabone Company, is constructed of strong polyurethane, which is softer than nylon. Less powerful chewers prefer the Gumabones® to the Nylabones®. A super option for your dog is the Hercules Bone®, a uniquely shaped bone named after the great Olympian for its

Rawhide can be dangerous and cause your dog to choke on it as it swells when wet. A new product, molded rawhide called Roar-Hide® by Nylabone®, is very safe for dogs.

exceptional strength. Like all Nylabone products, they are specially scented to make them attractive to your dog. Ask your veterinarian about these bones and he will validate the good doctor's prescription: Nylabones® not only give your dog a good chewing workout but also help to save your dog's teeth (and even his life, as it protects him from possible fatal periodontal diseases).

By the time dogs are four years old, 75% of them have periodontal disease. It is the most common infection in dogs. Yearly examinations by your veterinarian are essential to maintaining your dog's good health. If your veterinarian detects periodontal disease, he or she may recommend a prophylactic cleaning. To do a thorough cleaning, it will be necessary to put your dog under anesthesia. With modern gas anesthetics and monitoring

The chocolate Nylabone® has a one-micron-thick coat of chocolate under the skin of the nylon. When the Boxer chews it, the white subsurface is exposed.

equipment, the procedure is pretty safe. Your veterinarian will scale the teeth with an ultrasound scaler or hand instrument. This removes the calculus from the teeth. If there are calculus deposits below the gum line, the veterinarian will plane the roots to make them smooth. After all of the calculus has been removed, the teeth are polished with pumice in a polishing cup. If any medical or surgical treatment is needed, it is done at this time. The final step would be fluoride treatment and your follow-up treatment at home. If the periodontal disease is advanced, the veterinarian may prescribe a medicated mouth rinse or antibiotics for use at home. Make sure your dog has safe, clean and attractive chew toys and treats. Chooz® treats are another way of using a consumable treat to help keep your dog's teeth clean.

Rawhide is the most popular of all materials for a dog to chew. This has never been good news to dog owners, because rawhide is inherently very dangerous for dogs. Thousands of dogs have died from rawhide, having swallowed the hide after it has become soft and mushy, only to case stomach and intestinal blockage. A new rawhide product on the market has finally solved the problem of rawhide: molded Roar-Hide® from Nylabone. These are composed of processed, cut up, and melted American rawhide injected into your dog's favorite shape: a dog bone. These dog-safe devices smell and taste like rawhide but don't break up. The ridges on the bones help to fight tartar build-up on the teeth and they last ten times longer than the usual rawhide chews.

As your Boxer ages, a professional examination and cleaning of the teeth should become more frequent. The mouth should be inspected at least once a year.

As your dog ages, professional examination and cleaning should become more frequent. The mouth should be inspected at least once a year. Your veterinarian may recommend visits every six months. In the geriatric patient, organs such as the heart, liver, and kidneys do not function as well as when they were young. Your veterinarian will probably want to test these organs' functions prior to using general anesthesia for dental cleaning. If your dog is a good chewer and you work closely with your veterinarian, your dog can keep all of its teeth all of its life. However, as your dog ages, his sense of smell, sight, and taste will diminish. He may not have the desire to chase, trap or chew his toys. He will also not have the energy to chew for long periods, as arthritis and periodontal disease make chewing painful. This will leave you with more responsibility for keeping his teeth clean and healthy. The dog that would not let you brush his teeth at one year of age, may let you brush his teeth now that he is ten years old.

If you train your dog with good chewing habits as a puppy, he will have healthier teeth throughout his life.

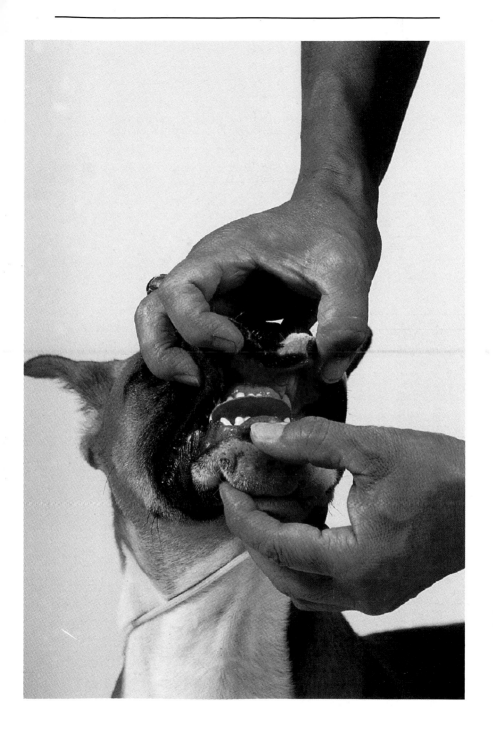

BEHAVIOR and Canine Communication

Studies of the human/animal bond point out the importance of the unique relationships that exist between people and their pets. Those of us who share our lives with pets understand the special part they play through companionship, service and protection.

Senior citizens show more concern for their own eating habits when they have the responsibility of feeding a dog. Seeing that their dog is routinely exercised encourages the owner to think of schedules that otherwise may seem unimportant to the senior citizen. The older owner may be arthritic and feeling poorly but with responsibility for his dog

The human/animal bond is the unique relationship that people share with their pets. This is Natalie Robbins and Australian Ch. Tobana Chattahoochee.

he has a reason to get up and get moving. It is a big plus if his dog is an attention seeker who will demand such from his owner.

Over the last couple of decades, it has been shown that pets relieve the stress of those who lead busy lives. Owning a pet has been known to lessen the occurrence of heart attack and stroke.

Many single folks thrive on the companionship of a dog. Lifestyles are very different from a long time ago, and today more individuals seek the single life. However, they receive fulfillment from owning a dog.

This is Ch. Sjecoin Winter forecast, a ten-an-half-year-old Boxer, with some neighborhood friends. Dogs teach children responsibility through understanding their care.

Most likely the majority of our dogs live in family environments. The companionship they provide is well worth the effort involved. In my opinion, every child should have the opportunity to have a family dog. Dogs teach responsibility through understanding their care, feelings and even respecting their life cycles. Frequently those children who have not been exposed to dogs grow up afraid of dogs, which isn't good. Dogs sense timidity and some will take advantage of the situation.

Today more dogs are serving as service dogs. Since the origination of the Seeing Eye dogs years ago, we now have trained hearing dogs. Also dogs are trained to provide service for the handicapped and are able to perform many different tasks for their owners. Search and Rescue dogs, with their handlers, are sent throughout the world to assist in recovery of disaster victims. They are life savers.

Therapy dogs are very popular with nursing homes, and some hospitals even allow them to visit. The inhabitants truly look forward to their visits. I have taken a couple of my dogs visiting and left in tears when I saw the response of the patients. They wanted and were allowed to have my dogs in their beds to hold and love.

Nationally there is a Pet Awareness Week to educate students and others about the value and basic care of our pets. Many countries take an even greater interest in their pets than Americans do. In those countries the pets are allowed to accompany their owners into restaurants and shops, etc. In the U.S. this freedom is only available to our service dogs. Even so we think very highly of the human/ animal bond.

CANINE BEHAVIOR

Canine behavior problems are the number-one reason for pet owners to dispose of their dogs, either through new homes, humane shelters or euthanasia. Unfortunately there are too many owners who are unwilling to devote the necessary time to properly train their dogs. On the other hand, there are those who not only are concerned about inherited health problems but are also aware of the dog's mental stability.

You may realize that a breed and his group relatives (i.e., sporting, hounds, etc.) show

Biting can be a problem for some puppies. If the puppy bites too hard, say "easy" and let him know he is hurting you. Owners, the Michals family.

132

Every child should have the opportunity of having a family dog. Owned by Verena Jaeger.

tendencies to behavioral characteristics. An experienced breeder can acquaint you with his breed's personality. Unfortunately many breeds are labeled with poor temperaments when actually the breed as a whole is not affected but only a small percentage of individuals within the breed.

If the breed in question is very popular, then of course there may be a higher number of unstable dogs. Do not label a breed good or bad. I know of absolutely awful-tempered dogs within one of our most popular, lovable breeds.

Inheritance and environment contribute to the dog's behavior. Some naïve people suggest inbreeding as the cause of bad temperaments. Inbreeding only results in poor behavior if the ancestors carry the trait. If there are excellent temperaments behind the dogs, then inbreeding will promote good temperaments in the offspring. Did you ever consider that inbreeding is what sets the characteristics of a breed? A purebred dog is the end result of inbreeding. This does not spare the mixed-breed dog from the same problems. Mixed-breed dogs frequently are the offspring of purebred dogs.

When planning a breeding, I like to observe the potential stud and his offspring in the show ring. If I see unruly behavior, I try to look into it further. I want to know if it is genetic or environmental, due to the lack of training and socialization. A good breeder will avoid breeding mentally unsound dogs.

Not too many decades ago most of our dogs led a different lifestyle than what is prevalent today. Usually mom stayed home so the dog had human companionship and someone to

Swimming can be great exercise for your Boxer. This is Jacquet's Mickey Mouse owned by Lucie Lecomte and Nicole Haineault.

discipline it if needed. Not much was expected from the dog. Today's mom works and everyone's life is at a much faster pace.

The dog may have to adjust to being a "weekend" dog. The family is gone all day during the week, and the dog is left to his own devices for entertainment. Some dogs sleep all day waiting for their family to come home and others become wigwam wreckers if given the opportunity. Crates do ensure the safety of the dog and the house. However, he could become physically and emotionally cripple if he doesn't get enough exercise and attention. We still appreciate and want the companionship of our dogs although we expect more from them. In many cases we tend to forget dogs are just that—*dogs* not human beings.

Boxers playing in the snow in Norway. Always try to make time to offer your dogs daily exercise time— winter is no exception.

I own several dogs who are left crated during the day but I do try to make time for them in the evenings and on the weekends. Also we try to do something together before I leave for work. Maybe it helps them to have the companionship of other dogs. They accept their crates as their personal "houses" and seem to be content with their routine and thrive on trying their best to please me.

SOCIALIZING AND TRAINING

Many prospective puppy buyers lack experience regarding the proper socialization and training needed to develop the type of pet we all desire. In the first 18 months, training does take some work. Trust me, it is easier to start proper training before there is a problem that needs to be corrected.

The initial work begins with the breeder. The breeder should start socializing the puppy at five to six weeks of age and cannot let up. Human socializing is critical up through 12 weeks of age and likewise important during the following months. The litter should be left together during the first few weeks but it is necessary to separate them by ten weeks of age. Leaving them together after that time will increase competition for litter dominance. If puppies are not socialized with people by 12 weeks of age, they will be timid in later life.

The eight- to ten-week age period is a fearful time for puppies. They need to be handled very gently around children and adults. There should be no harsh discipline during this time. Starting at 14 weeks of age, the puppy begins the juvenile period, which ends when he reaches sexual maturity around six

The eight-to-ten-week period is a fearful time for puppies. It is important to handle puppies gently and avoid harsh discipline around this time. Puppy bred by the author.

to 14 months of age. During the juvenile period he needs to be introduced to strangers (adults, children and other dogs) on the home property. At sexual maturity he will begin to bark at strangers and become more protective. Males start to lift their legs to urinate but if you desire you can inhibit this behavior by walking your boy on leash away from trees, shrubs, fences, etc.

Perhaps you are thinking about an older puppy. You need to inquire about the puppy's social experience. If he has lived in a kennel, he may have a hard time adjusting to people and environmental stimuli. Assuming he has had a good social upbringing, there are advantages to an older puppy.

Training includes puppy kindergarten and a minimum of one to two basic training classes. During these classes

Littermates should be left together for the first few weeks for proper socialization, but it is very beneficial to give them individual attention by ten weeks of age. Puppies bred by the author.

you will learn how to dominate your youngster. This is especially important if you own a large breed of dog. It is somewhat harder, if not nearly impossible, for some owners to be the Alpha figure when their dog towers over them. You will be taught how to properly restrain your dog. This concept is important. Again it puts you in the Alpha position. All dogs need to be restrained many times during their lives. Believe it or not, some of our worst offenders are the eight-week-old puppies that are brought to our clinic. They need to be gently restrained for a nail trim but the way they carry on you would think we were killing them. In comparison, their vaccination is a "piece of cake." When we ask dogs to do something that is not agreeable to them, then their worst comes out. Life will be easier for your dog if you expose him at a young age to the necessities of life—proper behavior and restraint.

UNDERSTANDING THE DOG'S LANGUAGE

Most authorities agree that the dog is a descendent of the wolf. The dog and wolf have similar traits. For instance both are pack oriented and prefer not to be isolated for long periods of time. Another characteristic is that the dog, like the wolf, looks to the leader—Alpha—for direction. Both the wolf and the dog communicate through body language, not only within their pack but with outsiders.

Every pack has an Alpha figure. The dog looks to you, or should look to you, to be that leader. If your dog doesn't receive the proper training and guidance, he very well may replace you as Alpha. This would be a serious problem and is certainly a disservice to your dog.

Eye contact is one way the Alpha wolf keeps order within his pack. You are Alpha so you must establish eye contact with your puppy. Obviously your puppy will have to look at you. Practice eye contact even if you need to hold his head for five to ten seconds at a time. You can give him a treat as a reward. Make sure your eye contact is gentle and not threatening. Later, if he has been naughty, it is permissible to give him a long, penetrating look. I caution you there are some older dogs that never learned eye contact as puppies and cannot accept eye contact. You should avoid eye contact with these dogs since they feel threatened and will retaliate as such.

Body Language

The play bow, when the forequarters are down and the hindquarters are elevated, is an invitation to play. Puppies play fight, which helps them learn the acceptable limits of biting. This is necessary for later in their lives. Nevertheless, an owner may be falsely reassured by the playful nature of his dog's aggression. Playful aggression toward another dog or human may be an indication of serious aggression in the future. Owners should

The play bow is an invitation for roughhousing, "boxing" and general fun. This is Ch. Tudossals Whizzard Of Laurel Hill owned by Jeannie and Bruce Korson.

never play fight or play tug-of-war with any dog that is inclined to be dominant. Signs of submission are:

1. Avoids eye contact.
2. Active submission—the dog crouches down, ears back and the tail is lowered.
3. Passive submission—the dog rolls on his side with his hindlegs in the air and frequently urinates.

Signs of dominance are:

1. Makes eye contact.
2. Stands with ears up, tail up and the hair raised on his neck.
3. Shows dominance over another dog by standing at right angles over it.

Dominant dogs tend to behave in characteristic ways such as:

1. The dog may be unwilling to move from his place (i.e., reluctant to give up the sofa if the owner wants to sit there).

2. He may not part with toys or objects in his mouth and may show possessiveness with his food bowl.

3. He may not respond quickly to commands.

4. He may be disagreeable for grooming and dislikes to be petted.

Dogs are popular because of their sociable nature. Those that have contact with humans during the first 12 weeks of life regard them as a member of their own species—their pack. All dogs have the potential for both dominant and submissive behavior. Only through experience and training do they learn to whom it is appropriate to show which behavior. Not all dogs are concerned with dominance but owners need to be aware of that potential. It is wise for the owner to establish his dominance early on.

Boxer puppies that have contact with humans during the first 12 weeks of life regard them as members of their own species—their pack. Puppy bred by the author.

A human can express dominance or submission toward a dog in the following ways:

1. Meeting the dog's gaze signals dominance. Averting the gaze signals submission. If the dog growls or threatens, averting the gaze is the first avoiding action to take—it may prevent attack. It is important to establish eye contact in the puppy. The older dog that has not been exposed to eye contact may see it as a threat and will not be willing to submit.

2. Being taller than the dog signals dominance; being lower signals submission. This is why, when attempting to make friends with a strange dog or catch the runaway, one should kneel down to his level. Some owners see their dogs become dominant when allowed on the furniture or on the bed. Then he is at the owner's level.

This is Ch. Benjamin of 5T's and owner Jo Thomson.

3. An owner can gain dominance by ignoring all the dog's social initiatives. The owner pays attention to the dog only when he obeys a command.

No dog should be allowed to achieve dominant status over any adult or child. Ways of preventing are as follows:

1. Handle the puppy gently, especially during the three- to four-month period.

2. Let the children and adults handfeed him and teach him to take food without lunging or grabbing.

3. Do not allow him to chase children or joggers.

4. Do not allow him to jump on people or mount their legs. Even females may be inclined to mount. It is not only a male habit.

5. Do not allow him to growl for any reason.

6. Don't participate in wrestling or tug-of-war games.

7. Don't physically punish puppies for aggressive behavior. Restrain him from repeating the infraction and teach an alternative behavior. Dogs should earn everything they receive from their owners. This would include sitting to receive petting or treats, sitting before going out the door and sitting to receive the collar and leash. These types of exercises reinforce the owner's dominance.

Young children should never be left alone with a dog. It is important that children learn some basic obedience

Some dogs feel distress when separated from their owners, known as separation anxiety. Owners should not make a big deal out of comings and goings. Owner, Verena Jaeger.

commands so they have some control over the dog. They will gain the respect of their dog.

FEAR

One of the most common problems dogs experience is being fearful. Some dogs are more afraid than others. On the lesser side, which is sometimes humorous to watch, my dog can be afraid of a strange object. He acts silly when something is out of place in the house. I call his problem perceptive intelligence. He realizes the abnormal within his known environment. He does not react the same way in strange environments since he does not know what is normal.

In order to avoid a dominance problem it is important to handle your Boxer puppy gently, especially during the three- to four-month period. This is Patti Ann Rutledge with Etta James.

On the more serious side is a fear of people. This can result in backing off, seeking his own space and saying "leave me alone" or it can result in an aggressive behavior that may lead to challenging the person. Respect that the dog that wants to be left alone and give him time to come forward. If you approach the cornered dog, he may resort to snapping. If you leave him alone, he may decide to come forward, which should be rewarded with a treat. Years ago we had a dog that behaved in this manner. We coaxed people to stop by the house and make friends with our fearful dog. She learned to take the treats and after weeks of work she overcame her suspicions and made friends more readily.

Some dogs may initially be too fearful to take treats. In these cases it is helpful to make sure the dog hasn't eaten for about 24 hours. Being a little hungry encourages him to accept the treats, especially if they are of the "gourmet" variety. I have a dog that worries about strangers since people seldom stop by my house. Over the years she has learned a cue and jumps up quickly to visit anyone sitting on the sofa. She learned by herself that all guests on the sofa were to be trusted friends. I think she felt more comfortable with them being at her level, rather than towering over her.

Dogs can be afraid of numerous things, including loud noises and thunderstorms. Invariably the owner rewards (by comforting) the dog when it shows signs of fearfulness. I had a terrible problem with my favorite dog in the Utility obedience class. Not only was he intimidated in the class but he was afraid of noise and afraid of displeasing me. Frequently he would knock down the bar jump, which clattered dreadfully. I gave him credit because he continued to try to clear it, although he was terribly scared. I finally learned to "reward" him every time he knocked down the jump. I would jump up and down, clap my hands and tell him how great he was. My psychology worked, he relaxed and eventually cleared the jump with ease. When your dog is frightened, direct his attention to something else and act happy. Don't dwell on his fright.

AGGRESSION

Some different types of aggression are: predatory, defensive, dominance, possessive, protective, fear induced, noise provoked, "rage" syndrome (unprovoked aggression), maternal and aggression directed toward other dogs. Aggression is the most common behavioral problem encountered. Protective breeds are expected to be more aggressive than others but with the proper upbringing they can make very dependable companions. You need to be able to read your dog.

Many factors contribute to aggression including genetics and environment. An improper environment, which may include the living conditions, lack of social life, excessive punishment, being attacked or frightened by an aggressive dog, etc., can all influence a dog's behavior. Even spoiling him and giving too much praise may be detrimental. Isolation and the lack of human contact or exposure to frequent teasing by children or adults also can ruin a good dog.

Lack of direction, fear, or confusion lead to

aggression in those dogs that are so inclined. Any obedience exercise, even the sit and down, can direct the dog and overcome fear and/or confusion. Every dog should learn these commands as a youngster, and there should be periodic reinforcement.

When a dog is showing signs of aggression, you should speak calmly (no screaming or hysterics) and firmly give a command that he understands, such as the sit. As soon as your dog obeys, you have assumed your dominant position. Aggression presents a problem because there may be danger to others. Sometimes it is an emotional issue. Owners may consciously or unconsciously encourage their dog's aggression. Other owners show responsibility by accepting the problem and taking measures to keep it under control. The owner is responsible for his dog's actions, and it is not wise to take a chance on someone being bitten, especially a child. Euthanasia is the solution for some owners and in severe cases this may be the best

It is important to allow your Boxer to come in contact with other dogs. Properly socialized dogs will not show aggression toward one another.

choice. However, few dogs are that dangerous and very few are that much of a threat to their owners. If caution is exercised and professional help is gained early on, then I surmise most cases can be controlled.

The Boxer is a sweet-tempered breed. This six-month-old pup is Cutter owned by Nell Marshall.

Some authorities recommend feeding a lower protein (less than 20 percent) diet. They believe this can aid in reducing aggression. If the dog loses weight, then vegetable oil can be added. Veterinarians and behaviorists are having some success with pharmacology. In many cases treatment is possible and can improve the situation.

If you have done everything according to "the book" regarding training and socializing and are still having a behavior problem, don't procrastinate. It is important that the problem gets attention before it is out of hand. It is

If you and your Boxer run into an aggressive dog, try to stay calm and continue on your way. Remember, a Boxer will protect his owner faithfully if the situation arises.

estimated that 20 percent of a veterinarian's time may be devoted to dealing with problems before they become so intolerable that the dog is separated from its home and owner. If your veterinarian isn't able to help, he should refer you to a behaviorist.

IDENTIFICATION and Finding the Lost Dog

There are several ways of identifying your dog. The old standby is a collar with dog license, rabies, and ID tags. Unfortunately collars have a way of being separated from the dog and tags fall off. I am not suggesting you shouldn't use a collar and tags. If they stay intact and on the dog, they are the quickest way of identification.

For several years owners have been tattooing their dogs. Some tattoos use a number with a registry. Here lies the problem because there are several registries to check. If you wish to tattoo, use your social security number. The humane shelters have the means to trace it. It is usually done on the inside of the rear thigh. The area is first shaved and numbed. There is no pain, although a few dogs do not like the buzzing sound. Occasionally tattooing is not legible and needs to be redone.

The newest method of identification is microchipping. The microchip is a computer chip that is no larger than a grain of rice. The veterinarian implants it by injection between the shoulder blades. The dog feels no discomfort. If your dog is lost and picked up by the humane society, they can trace you by scanning the microchip, which has its own code. Microchip scanners are friendly to other brands of microchips and their registries. The microchip comes with a dog tag saying the dog is microchipped. It is the safest way of identifying your dog.

FINDING THE LOST DOG

I am sure you will agree with me that there would be little worse than losing your dog. Responsible pet owners rarely lose their dogs. They do not let their dogs run free because they don't want harm to come to them. Not only that but in most, if not all, states there is a leash law.

Beware of fenced-in yards. They can be a hazard. Dogs find ways to escape either over or under the fence. Another fast exit is through the gate that perhaps the neighbor's child left unlocked.

Below is a list that hopefully will be of help to you if you need it. Remember don't give up, keep looking. Your dog is worth your efforts.

1. Contact your neighbors and put flyers with a photo on it in their mailboxes. Information you should include would be the dog's name, breed, sex, color, age, source of identification, when your dog was last seen and where, and your name and phone numbers. It may be helpful to say the dog needs medical care. Offer a *reward*.

2. Check all local shelters daily. It is also possible for your dog to be picked up away from home and end up in an out-of-the-way shelter. Check these too. Go in person. It is not good enough to call. Most shelters are limited on the time they can hold dogs then they are put up for adoption or euthanized. There is the possibility that your dog will not make it to the shelter for several days. Your dog could have been wandering or someone may have tried to keep him.

The newest method of identification is microchipping. The microchip is a computer chip that is no bigger than a grain of rice.

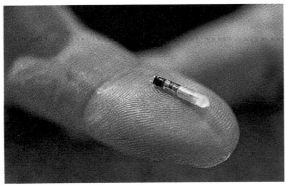

3. Notify all local veterinarians. Call and send flyers.

4. Call your breeder. Frequently breeders are contacted when one of their breed is found.

5. Contact the rescue group for your breed.

6. Contact local schools—children may have seen your dog.

7. Post flyers at the schools, groceries, gas stations, convenience stores, veterinary clinics, groomers and any other place that will allow them.

8. Advertise in the newspaper.

9. Advertise on the radio.

TRAVELING with Your Dog

The earlier you start traveling with your new puppy or dog, the better. He needs to become accustomed to traveling. However, some dogs are nervous riders and become carsick easily. It is helpful if he starts with an empty stomach. Do not despair, as it will go better if you continue taking him with you on short fun rides. How would you feel if every time you rode in the car you stopped at the doctor's for an injection? You would soon dread that nasty car. Older dogs that tend to get carsick may have more of a problem adjusting to traveling. Those dogs that are having a serious problem may benefit from some medication prescribed by the veterinarian.

Bosco owned by the Michals family seems to have found a comfortable seat in the car. Always consider the dog's safety and comfort when traveling.

Do give your dog a chance to relieve himself before getting into the car. It is a good idea to be prepared for a clean up with a leash, paper towels, bag and terry cloth towel.

The safest place for your dog is in a fiberglass crate, although close confinement can promote carsickness in some dogs. If your dog is nervous you can try letting him ride on the seat next to you or in someone's lap.

An alternative to the crate would be to use a car

Boxers love to travel! Ch. Merrilane's Monument, CD, Ch. Gabriela of Halakau, UD, and Ch. Seawest Choclatell Supriz, CD are enjoying a tidal pool vacation.

harness made for dogs and/or a safety strap attached to the harness or collar. Whatever you do, do not let your dog ride in the back of a pickup truck unless he is securely tied on a very short lead. I've seen trucks stop quickly and, even though the dog was tied, it fell out and was dragged.

I do occasionally let my dogs ride loose with me because I really enjoy their companionship, but in all honesty they are safer in their crates. I have a friend whose van rolled in an accident but his dogs, in their fiberglass crates, were not injured nor did they escape. Another advantage of the crate is that it is a safe place to leave him if you need to run into the store. Otherwise you wouldn't be able to leave the windows down. Keep in mind that while many dogs are overly protective in their crates, this may not be enough to deter dognappers. In some states it is against the law to leave a dog in the car unattended.

Never leave a dog loose in the car wearing a collar and leash. I have known more than one dog that has killed himself by hanging. Do not let him put his head out an open window. Foreign debris can be blown into his eyes. When leaving your dog unattended in a car, consider the temperature. It can take less than five minutes to reach temperatures over 100 degrees.

The Pet Safety Sitter is designed to protect dogs from injury by securing them in place and preventing them from disturbing drivers and passengers. Photo courtesy of Four Paws.

TRIPS

Perhaps you are taking a trip. Give consideration to what is best for your dog—traveling with you or boarding. When traveling by car, van or motor home, you need to think ahead about locking your vehicle. In all probability you have many valuables in the car and do not wish to leave it unlocked. Perhaps most valuable and not replaceable is your dog. Give thought to securing your vehicle and providing adequate ventilation for him. Another consideration for you when traveling with your dog is medical problems that may arise and little inconveniences, such as exposure to external parasites. Some areas of the country are quite flea infested. You may want to carry flea spray with you. This is even a good idea when staying in motels. Quite possibly you are not the only occupant of the room.

Crates are a safe way for your dog to travel. The fiberglass crates are safest but the metal crates allow more air.

Unbelievably many motels and even hotels do allow canine guests, even some very first-class ones. Gaines Pet Foods Corporation publishes *Touring With Towser*, a directory of domestic hotels and motels that accommodate guests with dogs. Their address is Gaines TWT, PO Box 5700, Kankakee, IL, 60902. I would recommend you call ahead to any motel that you may be considering and see if they accept pets. Sometimes it is necessary to pay a deposit against room damage. Of course you are more likely to gain accommodations for a small dog than a large dog. Also the management feels reassured when you mention that your dog will be crated. Since my dogs tend to bark when I leave the room, I leave the TV on nearly full blast to deaden the noises outside that tend to encourage my dogs to bark. If you do travel with your dog, take along plenty of baggies so that you can clean up after him. When we all do our share in cleaning up, we make it possible for motels to continue accepting our pets. As a matter of fact, you should practice cleaning up everywhere you take your dog.

Depending on where your are traveling, you may need an up-to-date health certificate issued by your veterinarian. It is good policy to take along your dog's medical information, which would include the name, address and phone number of your veterinarian, vaccination record, rabies certificate, and any medication he is taking.

AIR TRAVEL

When traveling by air, you need to contact the airlines to check their policy. Usually you have to make arrangements up to a couple of weeks in advance for traveling with your dog. The airlines require your dog to travel in an airline approved fiberglass crate. Usually these can be purchased through the airlines but they are also readily available in most pet-supply stores. If your dog is not accustomed to a crate, then it is a good idea to get him acclimated to it before your trip. The day of the actual trip you should withhold water about one hour ahead of departure and no food for about 12 hours. The airlines generally have temperature restrictions, which do not allow pets to travel if it is either too cold or too hot. Frequently these restrictions are based on the temperatures at the departure and arrival airports. It's best to inquire about a health certificate. These usually need to be issued within ten days of departure. You should arrange for non-stop, direct flights and if a commuter plane should be involved, check to see if it will carry dogs. Some don't. The Humane Society of the United States has put together a tip sheet for airline traveling. You can receive a copy by sending a self-addressed stamped envelope to:

The Humane Society of the United States
Tip Sheet
2100 L Street NW
Washington, DC 20037.

Regulations differ for traveling outside of the country and are sometimes changed without notice. Well in advance you need to write or call the appropriate consulate or agricultural department for instructions. Some countries have lengthy quarantines (six months), and countries differ in their rabies vaccination requirements. For instance, it may have to be given at least 30 days ahead of your departure.

Do make sure your dog is wearing proper identification. You never know when you might be in an accident and separated from your dog. Or your dog could be frightened and somehow manage to escape and run away. When I travel, my dogs wear collars with engraved nameplates with my name, phone number and city.

Another suggestion would be to carry in-case-of-emergency instructions. These would include the address and phone number of a relative or friend, your veterinarian's name, address and phone number, and your dog's medical information.

Ex pens are ideal when traveling. They provide off-lead exercise within safe and portable confines. Owners, Nancy and Bill Doyle.

BOARDING KENNELS

Perhaps you have decided that you need to board your dog. Your veterinarian can recommend a good boarding facility or possibly a pet sitter that will come to your house. It is customary for the boarding kennel to ask for proof of vaccination for the DHLPP, rabies and bordetella vaccine. The bordetella should have been given within six months of boarding. This is for your protection. If they do not ask for this proof I would not board at their kennel. Ask about flea control. Those dogs that suffer flea-bite allergy can get in trouble at a boarding kennel. Unfortunately boarding kennels are limited on how much they are able to do.

However daring and adventurous your Boxer may be, motorcycle travel is not recommended. This is Tim Teubner with Kayla's Breathless Way.

For more information on pet sitting, contact NAPPS:
National Association of Professional Pet Sitters
1200 G Street, NW
Suite 760
Washington, DC 20005.

Our clinic has technicians that pet sit and technicians that board clinic patients in their homes. This may be an alternative for you. Ask your veterinarian if he has an employee that can help you. There is a definite advantage of having a technician care for your dog, especially if your dog is on medication or is a senior citizen.

You can write for a copy of *Traveling With Your Pet* from ASPCA, Education Department, 441 E. 92nd Street, New York, NY 10128.

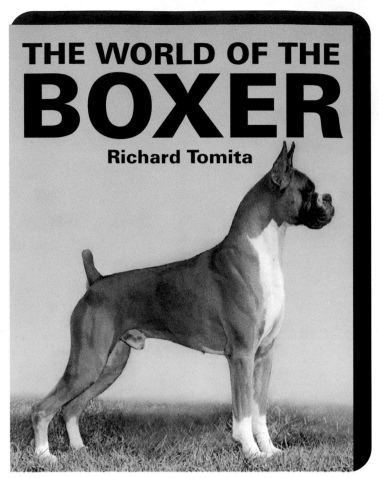

THE WORLD OF THE BOXER

Richard Tomita

TS-273

Highly regarded by the international dog community, Richard Tomita has assembled the most complete volume on the Boxer breed ever to be published. *The World of the Boxer* (TS-273) presents hundreds of the most important and influential Boxers, the kennels that produced them, and a comprehensive overview of the Boxer breed around the world. In addition to complete chapters on the United States, Australia, Canada and England, the author discusses Boxers in Germany and the Continent, as well as Japan, Brazil, India, Mexico, South Africa, and elsewhere. Chapters include showing and training the Boxer, history of the American Boxer Club, genetics, obedience, judging, and a special chapter on breeding, whelping and puppy care written as only this expert breeder can do. Over 1000 photographs grace this definitive volume, most of which are in color. No Boxer lover will do without this breed book masterpiece, an absolute essential for every Boxer library.

The Author welcomes your inquiries and comments and he can receive them at 5 Raritan Road, Oakland, NJ 07436.

SUGGESTED READING

TS-252
Dog Behavior and Training
288 pages, nearly 200 color photos.

TS-249
Skin & Coat Care for Your Dog
224 pages, 300 color photos.

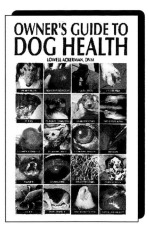

TS-214
Owner's Guide to Dog Health
432 pages, 300 color photos.

TS-205
Successful Dog Training
160 pages, 130 color photos.

TS-258
Training Your Dog For Sports and Other Activities
160 pages, over 200 color photos.

PS-813
The Boxer
256 pages, over 100 color photos.

INDEX